Enriching Our Worship 2

Ministry with the Sick or Dying
Burial of a Child

Supplemental Liturgical Materials

prepared by
The Standing Commission on Liturgy and Music

2000

✠ CHURCH

CHURCH PUBLISHING INCORPORATED, NEW YORK

Church Publishing Incorporated
445 Fifth Avenue
New York, NY 10016

5 4 3 2

Contents

Preface

From the Presiding Bishop and Primate

Enriching Our Worship 2 was developed by the Expansive Language Committee of the Standing Commission on Liturgy and Music in response to a resolution adopted by the 72nd General Convention in 1997. The resolution called on the Commission to develop supplemental liturgical materials for Pastoral Offices of the 1979 Book of Common Prayer. In reviewing the Prayer Book Pastoral Offices, the Commission realized there was a particular need to develop new prayers for ministry with those who are sick or dying, and to provide a rite for the burial of a child. They took on these tasks, and the fruit of their good efforts is contained in this volume.

Public services of healing have increasingly become part of the worship life of the Episcopal Church. What had been a private celebration of laying on of hands and anointing for healing (Visitation of the Sick) with the 1979 Book of Common Prayer has become a public service of healing in many congregations. *Enriching our Worship 2* includes litanies and prayers—some drawn from traditional prayers and others newly composed—to augment the Prayer Book service.

The new Pastoral Offices in this volume respond to tremendous changes over the past twenty-five years in ministry among those who are dying. The hospice movement and the development of palliative care units in hospitals and nursing home facilities highlight the changing climate of care for those who are at the end of life.

Advances in medical care and technology mean that the journey towards death in many instances has been extended, giving us a pastoral opportunity to share that journey. These medical advances have raised questions not only about prolonging life but also about withholding or discontinuing treatment, when the time comes. Prayers which take into account these new realities were developed in dialogue with our End of Life Issues Task Force.

Though the 1928 Book of Common Prayer introduced a rite for the Burial of a Child, none was included in the 1979 Prayer Book. The new rite of a Burial of a Child recognizes the pain and tragedy of the death of a child and God's loving protection and embrace of the innocent. In this collection there is a treasury of prayers that gives voice to our trust and faith in the living God.

I commend these enhancements of our common prayer in the hope that they will further our ability to respond to the needs of our people in such a way that they know the presence and power of Christ the compassionate one.

The Most Reverend Frank Tracy Griswold

Among the most powerful and poignant memories of parish priesthood are those involving end-of-life decisions, tragic deaths, and, especially, the deaths of children.

I remember too well the midnight visit to a couple whose gorgeous and vivacious three-year-old daughter had just died without warning. Only days before, the mother had told me that her little girl's smile and presence had changed the fortunes of the family, which previously had resembled Job's. Now, I stepped over a favorite rag doll, which she would never cuddle again.

I suppose I was helpful pastorally. The liturgy was good. Yet I still saw that little white casket in my dreams for some weeks afterward. How I wish that as a young priest I had had the wisdom and choices of *Enriching Our Worship 2: Ministry with the Sick or Dying and Burial of a Child*.

This excellent effort—which includes prayer with the sick, ministry with the sick and dying, a public service of healing, and preparation for death and dying—also identifies appropriate hymns and passages from scripture. It deals with the hard decisions of a faith, which understands that death is part of life even in a society whose technology seems to strive for immortality. It helps us to wrap the suffering, the decision-makers, and the loved ones in the great comfort and strength of the Body of Christ.

As a parish priest for many years, I often sought new works and new insights to serve our people in such times of crisis. Even those materials I liked were disappointing or more academic than real. These supplemental liturgical materials hit the mark. They are as practical and effective as they are comprehensive. The rich and powerful treasury of Christ's Church is opened to us in a new and striking way, whether we are lay or clergy. I heartily recommend them.

The Very Reverend George L.W. Werner

A Note About the Process

The 72nd General Convention directed the Standing Commission on Liturgy and Music to "develop supplemental liturgical materials for the Pastoral Offices of the Book of Common Prayer and to present those materials to the 73rd General Convention" (Resolution D086). The SCLM assigned this task to the Expansive Language Committee, chaired by Phoebe Pettingell.

At each Convention from 1985 through 1997, the General Convention has authorized the development and use of supplemental liturgical materials for the Holy Eucharist and Morning and Evening Prayer. The primary purpose of these materials has been to provide texts using inclusive and expansive language, that is, language which expands the images used to speak of and to God, and language in which all worshipers find themselves, and their religious experience of God as revealed in Christ, more completely reflected. These principles continue to inform the work of the Expansive Language Committee.

Mindful of the charge of the 72nd General Convention to consider "forms of worship reflective of our multicultural, multiethnic, multilingual and multigenerational Church while providing rites and structures that ensure the unity of Common Prayer" (C021s), the committee began its work by reviewing all the pastoral offices in the 1979 Book of Common Prayer. Under the guidance of the SCLM, the committee then focused its efforts on developing supplemental materials for Ministry with the Sick or Dying and for Burial of a Child.

In drafting these rites, the committee drew upon a wide range of sources: Scripture; contemporary prayerbooks of other churches of the Anglican Communion, including Canada, New Zealand, Australia, Scotland, Ireland, and South Africa; traditional materials from Orthodox and medieval western sources; and hymnody of different American cultures. Rather than borrowing directly from these sources, in most cases the committee has adapted material in order to craft prayers that will resonate with contemporary English-speaking Americans, including those who are not familiar with traditional liturgical language. A number of prayers have been newly written. Some texts from the 1979 Book of Common Prayer have been included; a few of these have been revised in order to update the language.

In addition to addressing concerns about inclusive and expansive language, the drafting committee was mindful of several other considerations:

◆ A number of parishes administer unction at the Sunday Eucharist, and healing services have become part of the life of many congregations. By using the structure of the Holy Eucharist as the basis of both A Public Service of Healing and Ministry in a Home or Health Care Facility, Ministry with the Sick or Dying sets the Church's ministry of healing in the context of the Church's principal act of worship on the Lord's Day.

◆ Both the 1928 and the 1979 Prayer Books moved away from an understanding of illness as divine punishment. These rites continue this development and proclaim the saving message of Jesus Christ.

◆ For Ministry in a Home or Health Care Facility and Ministration at the Time of Death, the committee has drafted texts with simple responses which can be used without everyone in the room having a Prayer Book.

♦ Advances in medical care since the 1979 rites were developed have resulted in situations where decisions are made about whether to continue the use of life-sustaining care. To respond to this pastorally, the committee developed "A Form of Prayer When Life-Sustaining Treatment is Withheld or Discontinued" based upon rites first prepared in the Diocese of Washington. In addition, these new materials provide pastoral direction on the need for Christians to prepare advance directives for health care.

♦ A broad range of collects, many of them newly written, address a number of different pastoral situations. Also included is a more extensive selection of prayers for use by those who are sick and prayers for use by children. Prayers that mention specific illnesses are not included in order that the rites not imply that some illnesses are of more concern to the Church.

♦ The 1979 Prayer Book eliminated a separate office for the Burial of a Child (which had been introduced in the 1928 Prayer Book). Pastoral experience since 1979 has indicated the desirability of a rite which responds to the particular dynamics of the death of a child.

To assist the committee in its work, a first draft of the new materials was circulated to a number of consultants, including professors of liturgy and pastoral theology at seminaries of the Episcopal Church, laity and clergy with extensive experience in pastoral care, and representatives of other Christian traditions. Responses from these consultants were taken into account as the committee refined the new materials.

Praying with the Sick

So I tell you, whatever you ask for in prayer,
  believe that you have received it, and it will be yours.

Mark 11:24

Since the needs of each individual situation and patient will be different, praying with the sick requires the greatest flexibility. Sometimes, the most familiar prayers, such as a well loved collect or the Lord's Prayer, the Prayer of St. Francis, or the 23rd Psalm will provide the most reassurance. On other occasions, extempore prayer or striking images from biblical sources may inspire and cheer. Sick persons often have little energy. It is therefore crucial to watch vigilantly for signs of fatigue, and not outstay the patient's stamina. The ill can be particularly vulnerable to jostling and to scents. The comfort of a touch will provide most solace when it is gentle. While the odors of anointing oils can have a powerful therapeutic effect, colognes and perfumes tend to be oppressive, sometimes to the point of respiratory distress.

In order to respond with sensitivity to the particular circumstances, those who have come to minister with the sick should prepare themselves in advance. Hands will be washed before the visit. If a service is to be conducted, readings and prayers will have been chosen beforehand and marked so that the effect will not be marred by needless flipping through pages.

Above all, those who pray with the sick need to be fortified by their own prayer life. Our effectiveness in intercession lies in our openness to the channels of God's healing grace. The wholeness we seek for others, we seek also for ourselves.

◆ "Praying *with* the sick seems more personal and penetrating than praying *for* the sick" [Norman Autton in *A Manual of Prayers and Readings for the Sick*, SPCK 1970]. Since illness is often accompanied by deep frustration, feelings of helplessness and loneliness, prayer which joins with patients can lift up and remind the afflicted that they are neither alone nor powerless in intercession, but are part of the whole communion of saints. Further, it reminds both them and the ministers that while some of us may appear to be healthy and full of life, sickness and death are universal conditions to which we all must come. Therefore, our prayer is an act of true sympathy and identification. St. Augustine wrote, "One becomes sick, oneself, to minister to the sick, not with any false claim to having the same fever, but by considering with an attitude of sympathy, how one would want to be treated if one were in the sick person's place."

◆ Prayers with the sick should be full of the *presence* and *power* of God. We are meeting with God about a particular situation, asking for help and guidance in sure and certain trust that while we cannot always understand, God's goodness will prevail in ways we cannot always know.

◆ Prayers with the sick will be positive. While relief is sought, lengthy enumerations of the patient's condition will add little. In *Letters to Malcolm*, C.S. Lewis remarked, "I have heard a man offer a prayer for a sick person which really amounted to a diagnosis followed by advice as to how God should treat the person." Yet positive prayers can be a fruitful opportunity to offer up the patient's negative feelings of anger or resentment (St. Teresa once prayed, "I do not wonder, God, that you have so few friends considering the way you treat them."). In this way, we acknowledge that all aspects of us belong to God. The words that shape our prayers will instill confidence. Since there continues to be a residue of older prayers and hymns suggesting that illness is judgment from God on the individual, care should be taken to avoid materials that convey a guilt-inducing theology which might undermine the sick person's confidence, breed feelings of worthlessness, and even interfere with recovery, rather than inspire a conviction of God's loving and compassionate presence.

◆ Praying with the sick will be filled with confident expectation that God hears us, and will answer. Of course, this does not mean that our own wishes will necessarily be granted. True healing comes about in closer communion with the heart of the Holy Trinity, regardless of physical or even psychological condition. On the other hand, we should not be timid in what we express, lest we imply that nothing positive may be expected. Prayers should be offered for the heart's desire, yet with spacious intention of living into God's will, rather than our offering shallow assurances.

◆ Prayers with the sick will be persistent. Patience becomes a necessity in illness. It is profoundly disheartening for patients to pray with people who expect their rapid recovery, only to become discouraged when the condition persists. In the case of chronic illnesses, one must sometimes cultivate a spirit hopeful enough to wait while temporarily accepting present circumstances. This protects the sick person from the peaks and valleys of raised hopes followed by frustration and disappointment. Again, the true nature of healing —which is our relationship and closeness with God—must be the focus of prayer. St. Augustine reminds us that even when God refuses the desires of our hearts he never refuses the heart of our desires.

◆ Praying with the sick may be costly. "It is so much easier to pray for a bore than to go and see him," C.S. Lewis wryly observed. When we take upon ourselves to join with the intercessions of others, we agree to share in their tribulations. We cannot remain aloof and detached. Lack of love on our part is quickly perceived in the sick room, where there are few distractions. When praying with those who are most vulnerable, our own preparation of heart will help us cultivate the compassion to identify with those we serve. We need protection lest we sit in judgment on low spirits, anger, nervousness, or self-pity. Our role with the sick is to witness to Christ's understanding of their condition.

Therefore, part of the act of prayer will entail listening to those we have come to visit. If we tell them instead how we think they ought to react, this will be perceived as rejection, and breed feelings of guilt, resentment, or worthlessness. It is up to us to recognize that physical and emotional tensions and pain often produce attitudes and behavior unexperienced or at least repressed in health. A sense of abandonment is common among those who have undergone a protracted illness, or one which has removed them from their previous activities. These people have the greatest need of the Church's community and acceptance.

◆ Healing must never be seen as an end in itself. Scripture teaches us that Jesus' healings were a sign of the reign of God come near, of God's marvelous power and presence among us. Healing is not merely the alleviation of affliction, but testimony to the wholeness and salvation God intends for us.

◆ Prayers with the sick will include periods of stillness. Silent prayer and meditation can instill a sense of peace which will be more useful than activity. The exhaustion sick people frequently experience makes them hypersensitive to fussing. "In quietness and confidence will be your strength." Our presence with the patient carries louder than spoken words. Hospitality requires that, when one prays with an unconscious or uncommunicative person, extra care should be taken to phrase thoughts and feelings in a gracious manner so that the one praying will not appear to be putting words into mouths unable to speak for themselves. Phrases such as "If there is anxiety, send your calm," bring more relief than "Help your anxious servant."

◆ Praise and thanksgiving are integral to prayer with the sick. Attention should ultimately focus on God rather than ourselves. A spirit of thankfulness will be quicker to appreciate the divine presence, and to hope and trust in God's nearness.

◆ Finally, all prayers with the sick should be linked with *the people of God* in the context of the whole Church. The community of intercessors embraces not only the parish, but also family and friends of the patients and all who are caring for them, as well as the medical community. At the same time, people long cut off from the outside world by illness and diminished stamina will inevitably have a vision of community different from those who lead active lives. Petitions should be tempered accordingly.

Our prayer is equally linked with the Passion of Christ, our loving intercessor who has taken on our suffering and redeemed us for our salvation, that we might come more fully into the wholeness of God's love.

Phoebe Pettingell
for the Standing Commission on Liturgy and Music

The organization and some of the principles outlined above have been adapted from *A Manual of Prayers and Readings for the Sick*, by Norman Autton [SPCK, 1970].

Ministry with the Sick or Dying

Ministry with the Sick or Dying

Introduction

In Ministry with the Sick or Dying, the Church acts in the grace of God for the health and salvation of its members. This ministry is based on Jesus' constant witness of concern and care for the sick. It is also shaped by the Epistle of James' direction to the sick to call for the elders of the Church to pray over them and anoint them with oil in the name of Jesus Christ (James 5:14). James expects these actions to have three effects: the prayer of faith will save the sick, the Lord will raise them up, and their sins will be forgiven.

We may draw two conclusions from our knowledge of early Christian ministry with the sick, as illustrated in Holy Scripture: first, Christians were to call on the senior members of their own community for prayer for healing; second, the ministry those leaders offered was an extension of the Church's basic act of worship: the proclamation of the Word and the offering of bread and wine each Sunday.

Sacramental healing is traditionally called "unction," defined by the Prayer Book as "the rite of anointing the sick with oil, or the laying on of hands, by which God's grace is given for the healing of spirit, mind, and body" (BCP p. 861). In Ministry with the Sick or Dying, healing is offered for any who feel the need for specific healing of spirit, mind, or body. While all Christians stand between the fullness of the baptismal gift of grace and the final consummation of that grace—and thus all are in need of healing—the sacrament is usually offered in response to some particular need or concern. The sacrament is particularly appropriate at times of discovery of illness, a turning point in an illness, a particular procedure, or at a time of great distress.

Traditionally, the oil used to anoint the sick is pure olive oil, blessed by a priest or bishop. Unlike the chrism used for baptismal anointing, no fragrance is added to oil for the sick (some fragrances can be allergens or aggravate an illness).

Prayer is also an important dimension of Ministry with the Sick or Dying. Some Christians, including some of the Church's great theologians and saints (such as John of the Cross, Julian of Norwich, and John Donne), have found illness to be a catalyst and stimulus for prayer. But many sick people find their prayer hampered by illness. The support of others in prayer becomes even more important in these times.

These new rites for Ministry with the Sick or Dying include public services of healing, the incorporation of sacramental healing in the context of a regular Sunday or weekday celebration of the Eucharist, and individual ministration in a home or health care facility. In addition, the suggested passages of scripture are appropriate for use by a sick person, and a number of prayers are included specifically for use by a sick person.

Order of Service

Ministry with the Sick or Dying may include some or all of the following actions by the minister and people. For both a Public Service of Healing and Ministry in a Home or Health Care Facility, the order of service follows that of the Sunday Eucharist. When prayer for healing precedes the liturgy of the table ("The Holy Communion," BCP pp. 333, 361), it is more evident that participation in communion is the climax of the service.

Gather in the Name of God

> The gathering may take the form of a greeting such as "Peace be to this house (place) and all who dwell in it." Suggestions are provided below for a public service of healing.

Proclaim and Respond to the Word

One or more passages of scripture may be read. When ministering to individuals, the minister may comment briefly on the reading. A public service of healing ordinarily includes a homily or other form of response, such as song, talk, dance, instrumental music, other art forms, silence. When Eucharist is to be celebrated (not administered from reserved sacrament), a reading from the Gospel is always included.

Pray for the World and the Church, particularly for God's healing grace

Prayer may be offered for individual(s) in need of healing and for the needs of the world and the Church. Laying on of hands [and anointing] is included as part of the Church's work of intercession, and the subsequent administration of communion is then focused on participation in the Sacrament of Christ's Body and Blood, which is the primary sacrament of healing. A confession of sin and absolution may be included prior to the laying on of hands. If communion is not included, the Lord's Prayer follows the laying on of hands.

Exchange the Peace

All present may greet one another in the name of Christ.

Participate in the Sacrament of Christ's Body and Blood

The Eucharist is the primary sacrament of healing to all who seek it. A public service of healing may include celebration of the Eucharist, beginning with the offertory, or may conclude after the exchange of the Peace. When communion is taken by a Lay Eucharistic Minister ("Lay Eucharistic Visitor") or an ordained minister to those who, by reason of illness or infirmity, are unable to participate in the Church's eucharistic assembly, those who are ill or infirm are enabled to experience their relation to the community and join their personal faith and witness to that of their community. Sometimes, especially in situations of lengthy confinement, the Eucharist may be celebrated in the home or health care facility; such on-site celebration of the Holy Eucharist for shut-in and seriously disabled persons may be an occasion of great joy and consolation.

Ministry with the Sick or Dying may conclude with a blessing. A public service of healing concludes with [a blessing and] a dismissal.

When unction is administered in the context of the Sunday Eucharist or a regular weekday Eucharist, the portion of "A Public Service of Healing" entitled "Laying on of Hands and Anointing" may be used. It is recommended that this take place immediately before the exchange of the Peace, so that it may be evident that participation in communion is the climax of the service.

Ministers of the Rites

Ministry with the Sick or Dying is under the direction of the Rector or other member of the clergy in charge of the local congregation.

Ordinarily, a priest or bishop presides at A Public Service of Healing. In the absence of a priest or bishop, a deacon or a lay reader may lead a service that includes the following:

Gather in the Name of God
Proclaim and Respond to the Word
Pray for the World and the Church
Laying on of Hands and Anointing

When a deacon or lay reader leads A Public Service of Healing, the liturgy concludes with the exchange of the Peace or with a dismissal.

At A Public Service of Healing, lay persons should read the lessons which precede the Gospel and may lead the Litany for Healing. A deacon should read the Gospel, may lead the Litany for Healing, and should perform the customary functions of diaconal assistance at the Lord's Table (BCP p. 354). In the absence of a deacon, an assisting priest may perform the diaconal functions.

Oil for anointing must be blessed by a priest or bishop.

Under the direction of the Rector or other member of the clergy in charge of the local congregation, lay persons with a gift of healing may administer or assist in administering the laying on of hands and anointing.

Ministry in a Home or Health Care Facility may be administered by an ordained or lay minister. If communion from the reserved sacrament is to be administered by a lay person, the guidelines for Lay Eucharistic Ministers are to be followed.

In case of serious illness, the member of clergy in charge of the congregation is to be notified immediately (BCP p. 453).

The Church's Teaching on Preparation for Death and Dying

Leaders of congregations have a responsibility to encourage their people to execute, review, and update advance directives for health care in the event that they might become unable to make and/or communicate decisions about their health care. Advance directives include both appointment of an agent to make health care decisions (e.g., "durable power of attorney for health care") and a direction as to the care to be received in the limited circumstance of being terminally ill with death imminent (e.g., "living will"). Ordained and lay leaders should encourage their people to develop such written advance directives in accordance with the requirements of their civil jurisdiction.

Traditionally, The Book of Common Prayer has taught (BCP p. 445) that the member of the clergy in charge of the congregation is to instruct the people of the duty of Christian parents to make prudent provision for the well-being of their families, especially for the nurture and custody of minor children; and of all people, while they are in health, to make wills with the aid of duly licensed legal counsel. Such instruments should provide for the disposal of temporal goods, and, if possible, provide bequests for religious and charitable uses.

A Public Service of Healing

This service is suitable for use in a congregation or other church setting. It may also be adapted as needed for use in a variety of settings, e.g., hospital, nursing home, or other health care facility.

When unction is administered in the context of the Sunday Eucharist or a regular weekday Eucharist, the portion of this service entitled "Laying on of Hands and Anointing" is used. It is recommended that this take place immediately before the exchange of the Peace.

Gather in the Name of God

The service may begin as appointed for a celebration of the Holy Eucharist, or with the Penitential Order, or with the following greeting

Minister   The grace of our Lord Jesus Christ, and the love of God, and the communion of the Holy Spirit, be with you all.

People   And also with you.

Minister   Let us pray.

After a period of silence, the Minister then says one of the following Collects, or some other appropriate Collect

Loving God, the comfort of all who sorrow, the strength of all who suffer: accept our prayers, and to those who seek healing [especially *N. and N.*, and all whom we name in our hearts], grant the power of your grace, that the weak may be strengthened, sickness turned to health, the dying made whole, and sorrow turned into joy; through Jesus Christ our Savior. *Amen.*

or this

God our healer, whose mercy is like a refining fire: by the loving-kindness of Jesus, heal us and those for whom we pray; that being renewed by you, we may witness your wholeness to our broken world; through Jesus Christ, in the power of the Spirit. *Amen.*

or this

Gracious God, we commend to your loving care all who suffer, especially those who come [here] seeking your healing grace [for themselves or others]. Give them patience and hope in their distress; strengthen and uphold them in mind and body; and grant, by your intervention, that all your people may be made whole according to your desire, through Jesus Christ, in the power of the Holy Spirit. *Amen.*

Proclaim and Respond to the Word

One or two Lessons are read before the Gospel.

Between the Lessons, and before the Gospel, a Psalm, hymn, or anthem may be sung or said.

The readings may be selected from the following list, or from "A Public Service of Healing" in The Book of Occasional Services, or from the Proper of the Day.

From the Old Testament

Job 7:1-4 (human beings have a hard service on earth)
Isaiah 35 (eyes shall be opened...ears unstopped...the lame shall leap)
Isaiah 38:1-5 (the healing of Hezekiah); see also 2 Kings 20:1-7
Isaiah 49:14-16 (I will not forget you)
Isaiah 53:4-6 (By his bruises we are healed)
Ezekiel 36:26-28 (a new heart and a new spirit)
Ezekiel 37:12-14 (I am going to open your graves)

Psalms 13; 23; 30; 71; 86:1-7; 103:1-5; 126; 145:14-22; 147:1-7

From the New Testament

Acts 3:1-10 (in the name of Jesus Christ...stand up and walk)
2 Corinthians 1:3-5 (God comforts us)
James 5:14-16 (is anyone among you sick?)
1 Peter 2:21-24 (by his wounds you have been healed)
1 John 5:13-15 (if we ask anything according to his will, he hears us)

The Gospel

Matthew 5:2-10 (Beatitudes); see also Luke 6:20-23
Matthew 8:5-10, 13 (healing centurion's servant); see also
    Luke 7:1-10
Matthew 8:14-17 (healing Peter's mother-in-law); see also
    Mark 1:29-34; Luke 4:38-41
Matthew 9:2-8 (your sins are forgiven); see also Mark 2:1-12;
    Luke 5:17-26
Matthew 11:28-30 (come to me all who are weary)
Mark 6:7, 12-13 (the disciples anointed many who were sick)
Mark 14:32-36 (not what I want, but what you want)
Luke 4:22-28 (do here also in your hometown the things you did
    at Capernaum)
Luke 8:41-56 (healing Jairus' daughter and woman with a
    hemorrhage); see also Matthew 9:18-26; Mark 5:21-43
Luke 13:10-13 (healing of woman crippled for eighteen years)
John 5:2-9 (take up your bed and walk)
John 6:47-51 (I am the Bread of Life)
John 21:18-19 (when you are old...)

Response to the Word

*A homily or other form of response, such as song, talk, dance, instrumental
music, other art forms, silence, may follow the Gospel.*

Pray for the World and the Church, particularly for God's healing grace

One of the following litanies may be used.

A Litany for Healing

The Deacon or other leader introduces the Litany with these or similar words

Let us name before God those for whom we offer our prayers.

The people offer names either silently or aloud.

The Leader continues with these or similar words (any of the indicated petitions may be omitted)

Let us offer our prayers for God's healing, saying, "Hear and have mercy"

(*or* "Answer our prayer" *or* "Have mercy").

Holy God, source of health and salvation,

Here and after each petition, the people respond

> Hear and have mercy
> *or*
> Answer our prayer
> *or*
> Have mercy.

Holy and Mighty, wellspring of abundant life,

Holy Immortal One, protector of the faithful,

Holy Trinity, the source of all wholeness,

Blessed Jesus, your Holy Name is medicine for healing and a promise of eternal life,

Jesus, descendant of David, you healed all who came to you in faith,

Jesus, child of Mary, you embraced the world with your love,

Jesus, divine physician, you sent your disciples to preach the Gospel and heal in your name,

Jesus our true mother, you feed us the milk of your compassion,

Jesus, Son of God, you take away our sin and make us whole,

Jesus, eternal Christ, your promised Spirit renews our hearts and minds,

Grant your grace to heal those who are sick, we pray to you, O God,

Give courage and faith to all who are disabled through injury or illness, we pray to you, O God,

Comfort, relieve, and heal all sick children, we pray to you, O God,

Give courage to all who await surgery, we pray to you, O God,

Support and encourage those who live with chronic illness, we pray to you, O God,

Strengthen those who endure continual pain, and give them hope, we pray to you, O God,

Grant the refreshment of peaceful sleep to all who suffer, we pray to you, O God,

Befriend all who are anxious, lonely, despondent, or afraid, we pray to you, O God,

Restore those with mental illness to clarity of mind and hopeful-ness of heart, we pray to you, O God,

Give rest to the weary, and hold the dying in your loving arms, we pray to you, O God,

Help us to prepare for death with confident expectation and hope of Easter joy, we pray to you, O God,

Give your wisdom and compassion to health care workers, that they may minister to the sick and dying with knowledge, skill, and kindness, we pray to you, O God,

Uphold those who keep watch with the sick, we pray to you, O God,

Guide those who search for the causes and cures of sickness and disease, we pray to you, O God,

Jesus, Lamb of God,

Jesus, bearer of our sins,

Jesus, redeemer of the world,

If the Lord's Prayer is not to be used elsewhere, it follows here.

The following Collect may be added

Compassionate God: You so loved the world that you sent us Jesus to bear our infirmities and afflictions. Through acts of heal-ing, he revealed you as the true source of health and salvation. For the sake of your Christ who suffered and died for us, con-quered death, and now reigns with you in glory, hear the cry of your people. Have mercy on us, make us whole, and bring us at last into the fullness of your eternal life. *Amen.*

A Litany of Healing

The Celebrant introduces the Litany with this bidding

Let us name before God those for whom we offer our prayers.

The People audibly name those for whom they are interceding.

A Person appointed then leads the Litany

God the Father, your will for all people is health and salvation;
We praise you and thank you, O Lord.

God the Son, you came that we might have life, and might have it
more abundantly;
We praise you and thank you, O Lord.

God the Holy Spirit, you make our bodies the temple of
your presence;
We praise you and thank you, O Lord.

Holy Trinity, one God, in you we live and move and have
our being;
We praise you and thank you, O Lord.

Lord, grant your healing grace to all who are sick, injured,
or disabled, that they may be made whole;
Hear us, O Lord of life.

Grant to all who seek your guidance, and to all who are lonely,
anxious, or despondent, a knowledge of your will and an awareness of your presence;
Hear us, O Lord of life.

Mend broken relationships, and restore those in emotional
distress to soundness of mind and serenity of spirit;
Hear us, O Lord of life.

Bless physicians, nurses, and all others who minister to the suffering, granting them wisdom and skill, sympathy and patience;
Hear us, O Lord of life.

Grant to the dying peace and a holy death, and uphold by the grace and consolation of your Holy Spirit those who are bereaved;
Hear us, O Lord of life.

Restore to wholeness whatever is broken by human sin, in our lives, in our nation, and in the world;
Hear us, O Lord of life.

You are the Lord who does wonders:
You have declared your power among the peoples.

With you, O Lord, is the well of life:
And in your light we see light.

Hear us, O Lord of life:
Heal us, and make us whole.

Let us pray.

A period of silence follows.

The Celebrant concludes the Prayers with one of the following or some other suitable Collect

Almighty God, giver of life and health: Send your blessing on all who are sick, and upon those who minister to them, that all weakness may be vanquished by the triumph of the risen Christ; who lives and reigns for ever and ever. *Amen.*

or this

Heavenly Father, you have promised to hear what we ask in the Name of your Son: Accept and fulfill our petitions, we pray, not as we ask in our ignorance, nor as we deserve in our sinfulness, but as you know and love us in your Son Jesus Christ our Lord. *Amen.*

or this

O Lord our God, accept the fervent prayers of your people; in the multitude of your mercies look with compassion upon us and all who turn to you for help; for you are gracious, O lover of souls, and to you we give glory, Father, Son, and Holy Spirit, now and for ever. *Amen.*

Confession of Sin

A Confession of Sin may follow, if it has not been said at the beginning of the service.

The Deacon or Celebrant says

Let us confess our sins to God.

Silence may be kept.

Minister and People

God of all mercy,
we confess that we have sinned against you,
opposing your will in our lives.
We have denied your goodness in each other,
   in ourselves,
   and in the world you have created.
We repent of the evil that enslaves us,
   the evil we have done,
   and the evil done on our behalf.
Forgive, restore, and strengthen us
through our Savior Jesus Christ,
that we may abide in your love
and serve only your will. Amen.

The Bishop when present, or the Priest, stands and says

Almighty God have mercy on you, forgive you all your sins through the grace of Jesus Christ, strengthen you in all goodness, and by the power of the Holy Spirit keep you in eternal life. *Amen.*

The Deacon or Celebrant says

Let us confess our sins against God and our neighbor.

Silence may be kept.

Minister and People

Most merciful God,
we confess that we have sinned against you
in thought, word, and deed,
by what we have done,
and by what we have left undone.
We have not loved you with our whole heart,
we have not loved our neighbors as ourselves.
We are truly sorry and we humbly repent.
For the sake of your Son Jesus Christ,
have mercy on us and forgive us;
that we may delight in your will,
and walk in your ways,
to the glory of your name. Amen.

The Bishop when present, or the Priest, stands and says

Almighty God have mercy on you, forgive you all your sins
through our Lord Jesus Christ, strengthen you in all goodness,
and by the power of the Holy Spirit keep you in eternal life.
Amen.

Confession of Need

*Instead of or in addition to the Confession of Sin, the following confession of
need may be used.*

The minister introduces the prayer with these or similar words

Let us confess our need for God's healing grace.

Silence

Minister and People

Compassionate God,
we confess our weaknesses and our need for your
    strengthening touch.
We confess that some illnesses stem from our own fault,
while others are beyond our control.
We turn to you, source of life,
and ask in the name of our Savior Jesus Christ
for the gifts of true healing and life in you. *Amen.*

Minister

May the God of love visit you in your times of trial and weakness, and raise you to newness of life, through Jesus Christ, in the power of the Holy Spirit. *Amen.*

Laying on of Hands and Anointing

If oil for the anointing of the sick is to be blessed, the priest or bishop says

Blessed are you, O God, source of life and health. In Jesus you became flesh and came to know the depth of human suffering. You sent the disciples to heal those who were sick. Sanctify this oil that all who are anointed with it may be healed, strengthened, and renewed, by the power of your Holy Spirit. *Amen.*

or this prayer of blessing

O Lord, holy Father, giver of health and salvation: Send your Holy Spirit to sanctify this oil; that, as your holy apostles anointed many that were sick and healed them, so may those who in faith and repentance receive this holy unction be made whole; through Jesus Christ our Lord, who lives and reigns with you and the Holy Spirit, one God, for ever and ever. *Amen.*

The minister may introduce the laying on of hands [and anointing] with these or similar words

Holy Scripture teaches us that Jesus healed many who were sick as a sign of the reign of God come near, and sent the disciples to continue this work of healing through prayer in his name, that the afflicted might be raised up and their sins forgiven, bringing them to eternal salvation. By laying hands upon the sick [and anointing them], the disciples witnessed to the marvelous power and presence of God. Pray that as we follow their example, we may experience Christ's unfailing love.

or this

The ministry of Jesus invites us to new life in God and with each other. In the laying on of hands [and anointing] we proclaim the Good News that God desires us to be healthy and one in the body of Christ. You are invited to offer yourself, whatever your sickness of spirit, mind, or body, and ask for healing and wholeness in the Name of the holy and undivided Trinity.

The minister may invite each person to be anointed to give her or his name and any particular request for prayer. The minister then lays hands upon the sick person [and anoints the person], prays silently, then prays aloud using one of the following forms or similar words

N., I lay my hands upon you [and anoint you]. Receive Christ's gift of healing [especially for __]. May the power of the Savior who suffered for you wash over you, that you may be raised up in peace and inward strength. *Amen.*

or this

N., I [anoint you and] lay my hands upon you in the name of God the holy and undivided Trinity. May Christ be present with you to comfort you, to guard and protect you, and to keep you in everlasting life. *Amen.*

or this

N., I lay my hands upon you [and anoint you] in the name of the Father, and of the Son, and of the Holy Spirit, praying that our Savior Jesus Christ will sustain you, drive away sickness of body and mind and spirit, and give you that victory of life and peace which will enable you to serve and rejoice in God both now and evermore. *Amen.*

or this

N., I lay my hands upon you [and anoint you] in the name of our Savior Jesus Christ, praying you will be strengthened and filled with God's grace, that you may know the healing power of the Spirit. *Amen.*

The minister may add, in these or similar words

As you are outwardly anointed with this holy oil, so may our loving God give you the inward anointing of the Holy Spirit. Of God's bounty, may your suffering be relieved, and your spirit, mind, and body restored to grace and peace. May all of us in the frailty of our flesh know God's healing and resurrecting power. *Amen.*

If communion is not to follow, the Lord's Prayer is said.

The Laying on of Hands [and Anointing] may conclude with one or more of the following Collects

May the God who goes before you through desert places by night and by day be your companion and guide; may your journey be with the saints; may the Holy Spirit be your strength, and Christ your clothing of light, in whose name we pray. *Amen.*

or this

May God who is a strong tower to all, to whom all things in heaven and on earth bow and obey, be now and evermore your defense, and help you to know that the name given to us for health and salvation is the Name of our Redeemer, Jesus Christ. *Amen.*

or this

Generous God, we give you thanks for your beloved Jesus Christ, in whom you have shared the beauty and pain of human life. Look with compassion upon all for whom we pray, and strengthen us to be your instruments of healing in the world, by the power of the Holy Spirit. *Amen.*

or this

Thank you, Holy One of Blessing, for the good work of healing already begun in your servant[s] *N.* Grant that *she/he/they* may wait upon you with an expectant heart and rise up in joy at your call; in Christ's name we pray. *Amen.*

The following may be added

God of all mercy: help us who minister with the sick and dying to remember that though we may appear healthy, we, too, suffer from the universal human condition in a fallen world. Flesh withers, and we must all die to the life we know. Therefore, O God our help, teach us to be aware of our own infirmities, the better to make others understand they are not alone in their illness. Restore us all in the love of the holy and undivided Trinity which is our true health and salvation. *Amen.*

Exchange the Peace

Here or elsewhere in the service, all present may greet one another in the name of Christ.

If the Eucharist is not to be celebrated, the service may conclude with the Exchange of the Peace or with a [Blessing and] Dismissal.

Participate in the Sacrament of Christ's Body and Blood

The service continues with the Offertory (BCP p. 361). Texts from Enriching Our Worship 1 *(pp. 57-71) may be used for the eucharistic prayer, fraction anthem, postcommunion prayer, and the Blessing. The following may be used for the postcommunion prayer, which is especially appropriate when Communion has been received in one kind.*

Faithful God
in the wonder of your wisdom and love
you fed your people in the wilderness with the bread of angels,
and you sent Jesus to be the bread of life.
We thank you for feeding us with this bread.
May it strengthen us
that by the power of the Holy Spirit
we may embody your desire
and be renewed for your service
through Jesus Christ our Savior. Amen.

Or the postcommunion prayer on p. 399 of the Book of Common Prayer *may be used.*

If a Blessing is desired before the Dismissal, the following may be used

May the God of peace sanctify you entirely, and may your spirit and soul and body be kept sound and blameless at the coming of our Lord Jesus Christ. *Amen.*
1 Thessalonians 5:23

or this

May the One who creates and restores everything that is,
the One who is Mary's child and child of God,
the One who is the Holy Spirit,
May this Holy One bring you compassion and peace,
and bless your lives with joy. *Amen.*

or this

May the God of hope fill us with every joy in believing.
May the peace of Christ abound in our hearts.
May we be enriched by the gifts of the Holy Spirit, now and for
ever. *Amen.*

Hymns Appropriate for Ministry with the Sick

The Hymnal 1982

S 190-197	The Song of Zechariah *Benedictus Dominus Deus* (Canticle 4)
S 196-200	The Song of Simeon *Nunc dimittis* (Canticle 5)
S217	The Second Song of Isaiah *Quaerite Dominum* (Canticle 10)
287	For all the saints, who from their labors rest
333	Now the silence
334	Lord, dismiss us with thy blessing
335	I am the bread of life
383, 384	Fairest Lord Jesus
439	What wondrous love is this
453	As Jacob with travel was weary one day
469, 470	There's a wideness in God's mercy
482	Lord of all hopefulness, Lord of all joy
487	Come, my Way, my Truth, my Life
490	I want to walk as a child of the light
517	How lovely is thy dwelling-place (Psalm *84*—Brother James' Air)
552, 553	Fight the good fight with all thy might
560	Remember your servants, Lord
593	Lord, make us servants of your peace
602	Jesu, Jesu, fill us with your love
645, 646	The King of love my shepherd is
662	Abide with me: fast falls the eventide
663	The Lord my God my shepherd is
676	There is a balm in Gilead

682	O God, our help in ages past
683, 684	O for a closer walk with God
707	Take my life, and let it be
711	Seek ye first the kingdom of God
712	Dona nobis pacem
714	Shalom, my friends

Wonder, Love, and Praise

727, st. 1	As panting deer desire the waterbrooks
740	Wade in the water
749	The tree of life my soul has seen
753, 754	When from bondage we are summoned
755	The steadfast love of the Lord never ceases
756	Lead me, guide me, along the way
764	Taste and see
765	O blessed spring
770	O God of gentle strength
772	O Christ, the healer, we come
773	Heal me, hands of Jesus
774	From miles around the sick ones came
775	Give thanks for life
776	No saint on earth lives life to self alone
787	We are marching in the light of God
800	Precious Lord, take my hand
801	God be with you till we meet again
804	Steal away
805	I want Jesus to walk with me
810	You who dwell in the shelter of the Lord (Eagle's wings)
812	I, the Lord of sea and sky
813	Way, way, way
820	The eyes of all wait upon you
826	Stay with me
827	O Lord hear my pray'r
881, 882	The First Song of Isaiah *Ecce, Deus* (Canticle 9)

Lutheran Book of Worship

474   Children of the heav'nly Father

Voices United (United Church of Canada)

684   Make me a channel of your peace

Ministry in a Home or Health Care Facility

The many different situations in which this rite may be administered call for careful preparation. What are the particular needs and circumstances of the individual(s) being visited? How long can the sick person focus and be engaged in ritual action? Where is this individual in the course of illness and treatment? Will caregivers be present? Will family and/or friends be present? It is appropriate to consider such matters when deciding which portions of the service to include and selecting collects and readings.

In liturgical tradition, the presiding minister often washes hands ceremonially during the preparation of the altar/table. When visiting the sick at home or in a health care facility, it takes on an added hygienic importance. It is always appropriate to wash hands before and after a visit.

What special plans are needed for administration of the sacrament? Will a communion spoon be needed? Is the patient in protective isolation which requires sterilization of the eucharistic element?

In ministry with the sick, one or more parts of the following rite are used, as appropriate to the situation. When two or more parts are used together, they are used in the order indicated. The Lord's Prayer is always included.

Gather in the Name of God

The Minister begins the service with the following or some other greeting

Peace be to this house (place) and all who dwell in it.

or this

The grace of our Lord Jesus Christ, and the love of God, and the communion of the Holy Spirit, be with you all.

The Minister may continue with a Collect, beginning with

	The Lord be with you.
People	And also with you.
Minister	Let us pray.

After a period of silence, the Minister then says one of the following Collects, or some other appropriate Collect

Loving God, the comfort of all who sorrow, the strength of all who suffer: accept our prayers, and to those who seek healing, especially N. [*and N.*], grant the power of your grace, that the weak may be strengthened, sickness turned to health, the dying made whole, and sorrow turned into joy; through Jesus Christ our Savior. *Amen.*

or this

Gracious God, we commend to your loving care all who suffer, especially N. [*and N.*]. Give *him/her/them* patience and hope in distress; strengthen and uphold *him/her/them* in mind and body; and grant, by your intervention, that all your people may be made whole according to your desire, through Jesus Christ, in the power of the Holy Spirit. *Amen.*

or this

O God of peace, you have taught us that in returning and rest we shall be saved, in quietness and confidence shall be our strength. By the might of your Spirit lift us, we pray, to your presence, where we may be still and know that you are God; through Jesus Christ our Lord. *Amen.*

Proclaim and Respond to the Word

One or more of the following passages of scripture may be read

From the Old Testament

Job 7:1-4 (human beings have a hard service on earth)
Isaiah 35 (eyes shall be opened...ears unstopped...the lame shall leap)
Isaiah 38:1-5 (the healing of Hezekiah); see also 2 Kings 20:1-7
Isaiah 49:14-16 (I will not forget you)
Isaiah 53:4-6 (By his bruises we are healed)
Ezekiel 36:26-28 (a new heart and a new spirit)
Ezekiel 37:12-14 (I am going to open your graves)

Psalms 13; 23; 30; 71; 86:1-7; 103:1-3; 126; 145:14-22; 147:1-7

From the New Testament

Acts 3:1-10 (in the name of Jesus Christ...stand up and walk)
2 Corinthians 1:3-5 (God comforts us)
James 5:14-16 (is anyone among you sick?)
1 Thessalonians. 5:23-24 (may your spirit and soul and body be kept sound)
1 Peter 2:21-24 (by his wounds you have been healed)
1 John 5:13-15 (if we ask anything according to his will, he hears us)

Matthew 5:2-10 (Beatitudes); see also Luke 6:20-23
Matthew 8:5-10, 13 (healing centurion's servant); see also
    Luke 7:1-10
Matthew 8:14-17 (healing Peter's mother-in-law); see also
    Mark 1:29-34; Luke 4:38-41
Matthew 9:2-8 (your sins are forgiven); see also Mark 2:1-12;
    Luke 5:17-26
Matthew 11:28-30 (come to me all who are weary)
Mark 6:7, 12-13 (the disciples anointed many who were sick)
Mark 14:32-36 (not what I want, but what you want)
Luke 4:22-28 (do here also in your hometown the things you did
    at Capernaum)
Luke 8:41-56 (healing Jairus' daughter and woman with a
    hemorrhage); see also Matthew 9:18-26; Mark 5:21-43
Luke 13:10-13 (healing of woman crippled for eighteen years)
John 5:2-9 (take up your bed and walk)
John 6:47-51 (I am the Bread of Life)
John 21:18-19 (when you are old...)

The minister may comment briefly on the reading.

Pray for the World and the Church, particularly for God's healing grace

One or more of the "Prayers for Those Who are Sick" (pp. 64-70) or
"Additional Prayers" (pp. 93-95) may be used here.

The following general confession of sin and absolution may be said

Confession of Sin

A Confession of Sin may follow, if it has not been said at the beginning of the service.

The Deacon or Celebrant says

Let us confess our sins to God.

Silence may be kept.

Minister and People

God of all mercy,
we confess that we have sinned against you,
opposing your will in our lives.
We have denied your goodness in each other,
   in ourselves,
   and in the world you have created.
We repent of the evil that enslaves us,
   the evil we have done,
   and the evil done on our behalf.
Forgive, restore, and strengthen us
through our Savior Jesus Christ,
that we may abide in your love
and serve only your will. Amen.

The Bishop when present, or the Priest, stands and says

Almighty God have mercy on your, forgive you, forgive you all your sins through the grace of Jesus Christ, strengthen you in all goodness, and by the power of the Holy Spirit keep you in eternal life. *Amen.*

or this

The Deacon or Celebrant says

Let us confess our sins against God and our neighbor.

Silence may be kept.

Most merciful God,
we confess that we have sinned against you
in thought, word, and deed,
by what we have done,
and by what we have left undone.
We have not loved you with our whole heart;
we have not loved our neighbors as ourselves.
We are truly sorry and we humbly repent.
For the sake of your Son Jesus Christ,
have mercy on us and forgive us;
that we may delight in your will,
and walk in your ways,
to the glory of your name. Amen.

The Bishop when present, or the Priest, stands and says

Almighty God have mercy on you, forgive you all your sins
through our Lord Jesus Christ, strengthen you in all goodness, and
by the power of the Holy Spirit keep you in eternal life. *Amen.*

Confession of Need

*Instead of or in addition to the Confession of Sin, the following confession of
need may be used*

The minister introduces the prayer with these or similar words

Let us confess our need for God's healing grace.

Silence

Minister and People

Compassionate God,
we confess our weaknesses and our need for your strengthening touch.
We confess that some illnesses stem from our own fault,
while others are beyond our control.

We turn to you, source of life,
and ask in the name of our Savior Jesus Christ
for the gifts of true healing and life in you. *Amen.*

Minister

May the God of love visit you in your times of trial and weakness,
and raise you to newness of life, through Jesus Christ, in the
power of the Holy Spirit. *Amen.*

Laying on of Hands and Anointing

*Laying on of hands and anointing may be administered by a lay or ordained
minister. If the person is to be anointed, the oil must have been previously
blessed by a priest or bishop.*

*The minister may introduce the laying on of hands [and anointing] with the fol-
lowing or similar words; this is most appropriate when visitors are present for
the rite or if a person has not been previously anointed.*

Holy Scripture teaches us that Jesus healed many who were sick
as a sign of the reign of God come near, and sent the disciples to
continue this work of healing through prayer in his name, that
the afflicted might be raised up and their sins forgiven, bringing
them to eternal salvation. By laying hands upon the sick [and
anointing them], the disciples witnessed to the marvelous power
and presence of God. Pray that as we follow their example, we
may experience Christ's unfailing love.

*The minister may invite each person to be anointed to give her or his name and
any particular request for prayer. The minister then lays hands upon the sick
person [and anoints the person], prays silently, then prays aloud using one of the
following forms or similar words.*

N., I lay my hands upon you [and anoint you]. Receive Christ's
gift of healing [especially for _____]. May the power of the Savior
who suffered for you wash over you, that you may be raised up
in peace and inward strength. *Amen.*

or this

N., I [anoint you and] lay my hands upon you in the name of
God the holy and undivided Trinity. May Christ be present with
you to comfort you, to guard and protect you, and to keep you in
everlasting life. *Amen.*

or this

N., I lay my hands upon you [and anoint you] in the name of the
Father, and of the Son, and of the Holy Spirit, praying that our
Savior Jesus Christ will sustain you, drive away sickness of body
and mind and spirit, and give you that victory of life and peace
which will enable you to serve and rejoice in God both now and
evermore. *Amen.*

or this

N., I lay my hands upon you [and anoint you] in the name of our
Savior Jesus Christ, praying you will be strengthened and filled
with God's grace, that you may know the healing power of the
Spirit. *Amen.*

The minister may add, in these or similar words

As you are outwardly anointed with this holy oil, so may our loving
God give you the inward anointing of the Holy Spirit. Of God's
bounty, may your suffering be relieved, and your spirit, mind, and
body restored to grace and peace. May all of us in the frailty of our
flesh know God's healing and resurrecting power. *Amen.*

If Communion is not to follow, the Lord's Prayer is said.

*The Laying on of Hands [and Anointing] may conclude with one or more of the
following Collects*

May the God who goes before you through desert places by night
and by day be your companion and guide; may your journey be
with the saints; may the Holy Spirit be your strength, and Christ
your clothing of light, in whose name we pray. *Amen.*

or this

May God who is a strong tower to all, to whom all things in heaven and on earth bow and obey, be now and evermore your defense and help you to know that the name given to us for health and salvation is the Name of our Redeemer, Jesus Christ. *Amen.*

or this

Generous God, we give you thanks for your beloved Jesus Christ, in whom you have shared the beauty and pain of human life. Look with compassion upon all for whom we pray, and strengthen us to be your instruments of healing in the world, by the power of the Holy Spirit. *Amen.*

or this (especially appropriate during a time of recovery)

Thank you, Holy One of Blessing, for the good work of healing already begun in your servant N. Grant that *she/he* may wait upon you with an expectant heart and rise up in joy at your call; in Christ's name we pray. *Amen.*

or this (especially appropriate for one who is dying)

Hear the prayers of your child who desires to enter into your rest; grant that *she/he* may bear the pains of *her/his* body with fortitude, rest secure in your everlasting arms, and at last feast with your saints in light. *Amen.*

Exchange the Peace

Here or elsewhere in the service, all present may greet one another in the name of Christ.

Participate in the Sacrament of Christ's Body and Blood

If the Eucharist is to be celebrated, the Priest or Bishop begins with the Offertory.

If Communion is to be administered from the reserved Sacrament, the service continues with the Lord's Prayer, the minister first saying

As our Savior Christ
has taught us,
we now pray,

Our Father in heaven,
   hallowed be your Name,
   your kingdom come,
   your will be done,
     on earth as in heaven.
Give us today our daily bread.
Forgive us our sins
  as we forgive those
  who sin against us.
Save us from the time of trial,
  and deliver us from evil.
For the kingdom, the power,
  and the glory are yours,
  now and for ever. Amen.

And now, as our Savior
Christ has taught us,
we are bold to say,

Our Father, who art in heaven,
   hallowed be thy Name,
   thy kingdom come,
   thy will be done,
     on earth as it is in heaven.
Give us this day our daily bread.
And forgive us our trespasses,
  as we forgive those
  who trespass against us.
And lead us not into temptation,
  but deliver us from evil.
For thine is the kingdom,
  and the power, and the glory
  for ever and ever. Amen.

The minister may say the following Invitation

The Gifts of God for the People of God.

and may add

Take them in remembrance that Christ died for you, and feed on him in your heart[s] by faith, with thanksgiving.

The Sacrament is administered with the following or other words

The Body (Blood) of our Lord Jesus Christ keep you in everlasting life. [*Amen.*]

If the person cannot receive both the consecrated Bread and the Wine, it is suitable to administer the Sacrament in one kind only.

One of the usual postcommunion prayers is then said, or the following

Gracious Father, we give you praise and thanks for this Holy Communion of the Body and Blood of your beloved Son Jesus Christ, the pledge of our redemption; and we pray that it may bring us forgiveness of our sins, strength in our weakness, and everlasting salvation; through Jesus Christ our Lord. *Amen.*

or this

Faithful God
in the wonder of your wisdom and love
you fed your people in the wilderness with the bread of angels,
and you sent Jesus to be the bread of life.
We thank you for feeding us with this bread.
May it strengthen us
that by the power of the Holy Spirit
we may embody your desire
and be renewed for your service
through Jesus Christ our Savior. Amen.

If a person desires Communion but is unable to eat and drink the Bread and Wine, by reason of extreme sickness or disability, the minister should assure that person that all benefits of Communion are received through an act of spiritual communion even if the Sacrament is not received with the mouth. The minister [and/or the individual who is ill] may pray, using these or similar words

Faithful God,
in the wonder of your wisdom and love
you fed your people in the wilderness with the bread of angels,
and you sent Jesus to be the bread of life.
Though *N.* [*I*] cannot consume these gifts of bread and wine,
we [*I*] thank you that *he/she has* [*I have*] received the sacrament

of Christ's presence,
the forgiveness of sins, and all other benefits of Christ's passion.
By the power of the Holy Spirit,
may *we* [*I*] embody your desire
and be renewed for your service.
through Jesus Christ our Savior. *Amen.*

or this

God of infinite mercy,
we thank you for Jesus our Savior, our true Mother
who feeds us and gives us eternal life.
Though *N.* [*I*] cannot consume these gifts of bread and wine,
we [*I*] thank you that *he/she has* [*I have*] received the sacrament
   of Christ's presence,
the forgiveness of sins, and all other benefits of Christ's passion.
Grant that we may continue for ever in the Risen Life of our Savior,
who with you and the Holy Spirit,
lives and reigns, one God, now and for ever. *Amen.*

*The service concludes with a Blessing and/or with a Dismissal. One of the
following may be used.*

May the God of peace sanctify you entirely, and may your spirit
and soul and body be kept sound and blameless at the coming of
our Lord Jesus Christ. *Amen.*
1 Thessalonians 5:23

or this

After you have suffered for a little while, the God of all grace
who has called you to eternal glory in Christ, will restore, support,
strengthen, and establish you. To God be power for ever and ever.
Amen.
1 Peter 5:10

or this

May the God of hope fill you with every joy in believing.
May the peace of Christ abound in your heart.
May you be enriched by the gifts of the Holy Spirit,
    now and for ever. *Amen.*

Let us bless the Lord.
Thanks be to God.

Distribution of Holy Communion
by Lay Eucharistic Ministers
to persons who are ill or infirm

Concerning the Rite

The Book of Common Prayer affirms the place of the Holy Eucharist as "the principal act of Christian worship on the Lord's Day and other major Feasts," and thus the foundation of the corporate prayer of the Church. As an act of the whole community of faith, the Eucharist is a summons to all the baptized to share in the table of the Lord. This form for the distribution of Holy Communion by licensed lay persons is intended to foster a corporate sense of the Eucharist among those who, by reason of illness or infirmity, are unable to be present in their church's assembly on Sunday or some other principal feast.

This service is to be conducted by a duly licensed person immediately following such parish celebrations of the Holy Eucharist. Title III, Canon 3: Sec. 5(a) specifies that:

A Lay Eucharistic Minister is a person licensed to this extraordinary ministry. The Lay Eucharistic Minister shall have one or both of the following functions, as specified in the license:

(1) Administering the elements at any Celebration of Holy Eucharist in the absence of a sufficient number of Priests or Deacons assisting the celebrant;

(2) Directly following a Celebration of the Holy Eucharist on Sunday or other regularly scheduled Celebrations, taking the Sacrament consecrated at the Celebration to members of the Congregation who, by reason of illness or infirmity, were unable to be present at the Celebration. Persons so licensed may also be known as "Lay Eucharistic Visitors."

It is desirable that other parishioners, relatives, and friends also be present to communicate with the person visited. Those so ministered to should also be visited regularly by the clergy of the congregation. In this way, those who are unable to participate regularly in the worship of the eucharistic assembly may nevertheless experience their relation to the community and also join their personal faith and witness to that of their community. It is appropriate that the person be invited to join in commenting on the Scripture and in offering suitable prayers during the rite.

This form is to be used only immediately after regularly scheduled Celebrations.

The Lay Eucharistic Minister should be accompanied by other persons from the congregation.

The Lay Eucharistic Minister greets the people

The Peace of the Lord be always with you.
People   And also with you.

Collect of the Day

Gospel of the Day, or some other passage of Scripture appropriate to the occasion.

Comments may be made about the sermon of that day.

Suitable prayers may be offered.

A Confession of Sin may be said

Most merciful God,
we confess that we have sinned against you
in thought, word, and deed,
by what we have done,
and by what we have left undone.
We have not loved you with our whole heart;
we have not loved our neighbors as ourselves.

We are truly sorry and we humbly repent.
For the sake of your Son Jesus Christ,
have mercy on us and forgive us;
that we may delight in your will,
and walk in your ways,
to the glory of your Name. *Amen.*

Minister   May Almighty God in mercy receive our confession of
sorrow and of faith, strengthen us in all goodness, and
by the power of the Holy Spirit keep us in eternal life.
Amen.

The Lord's Prayer

Administration of the Holy Communion

(using one of the authorized words of administration)

Closing Prayer

O gracious God, whose Christ stretched out arms of love upon
the hard wood of the cross to embrace all the peoples of the
earth: We give you thanks for feeding N. our *sister* with the
Sacrament of that precious Body and Blood, which is the sign and
instrument of our common life, and also for enriching our parish
family by *her* sharing with us the food of our pilgrimage, the
foretaste of that heavenly banquet of which we shall partake with
all your saints; through Jesus Christ, our Savior. *Amen.*

Minister   Let us bless the Lord.
People   Thanks be to God.

Lay Eucharistic Ministers
specially licensed to take the Sacrament
to those who are ill or infirm

Suggested Guidelines

1. Lay Eucharistic Ministers must be adult confirmed communicants
   in good standing, be carefully chosen and trained, and be
   specially licensed. A candidate is to be recommended by the
   cleric in charge of the congregation to the Bishop of the diocese
   to be licensed. "A license shall be given only at the request,
   and upon the recommendation, of the Member of the Clergy
   in charge of the Congregation in which the person will be
   serving. The license shall be issued for a period of time not to
   exceed three years and shall be revocable by the Bishop, or by
   the Member of the Clergy in charge of the Congregation"
   (Title III, Canon 3, Sec. 2).

2. Where a Deacon serves in a congregation, that minister should
   supervise the work of the Lay Eucharistic Ministers.

3. It is recommended that the person to be ministered to be
   prayed for specifically in the Prayers of the People by the congregation on that day.

4. The administration of the Sacrament to the persons visited
   should take place immediately after the service in the church.
   Following the communion of the people, the Lay Eucharistic
   Ministers come forward and are commended for this ministry
   with the following or similar words:
   > In the name of this congregation, I send you forth bearing
   > these holy gifts, that those to whom you go may share with us
   > in the communion of Christ's body and blood. We who are
   > many are one body, because we all share one bread, one cup.

5. A suitable container in which to carry the two vessels for the bread and wine, corporals, and purificators is to be supplied. The container is to be returned immediately to the parish along with any unconsumed elements.

6. The people to whom Holy Communion is to be administered are to be notified in advance and the time of the appointment clearly set.

7. Only the order of the rite entitled "Distribution of Holy Communion by Lay Eucharistic Ministers" is to be used.

Prayers for Those Who are Sick

Any of the following prayers may be adapted as needed.

For Health of Body and Soul

May God the Father bless you, God the Son heal you, God the Holy Spirit give you strength. May God the holy and undivided Trinity guard your body, save your soul, and bring you safely to his heavenly country; where he lives and reigns for ever and ever. *Amen.*

For a Child

Heavenly Father, watch with us over your child N., and hear our yearning that *she/he* may be restored to health; through Jesus Christ our Redeemer. *Amen.*

or this

Gentle Jesus, stay beside your child N. through this day/night. Take away *her/his* pain. Keep *her/him* safe. Help *her/him* in *her/his* fear. Make *her/his* body strong again and *her/his* heart glad. Thank you for your love which surrounds *her/him* always. *Amen.*

or this

Jesus, our Redeemer, Good Shepherd of the sheep, you gather the lambs and carry them in your arms: We entrust our child N. to your loving care. Relieve *her/his* pain, restore in *her/him* your gifts of joy and strength, and raise *her/him* up to a life in your service. Hear us, we pray, for your dear Name's sake. *Amen.*

For a Visit with Someone Who is Sick

Gentle Jesus, though we are not worthy to have you come under our roof, you are God's word of healing to us. Be with us now, that we may know your presence in one another and rise up in joy to greet you. Grant this for your love's sake. *Amen.*

For Release

Blessed Jesus, Living Water, Solid Rock: Uphold your child N.; loose the fetters of sickness, break *her/his* yoke of pain, and from this land of affliction, lead *her/him* home. *Amen.*

For People with Diseases for Which There is No Cure

Loving God, your heart overflows with compassion for your whole creation. Pour out your Spirit on all persons living with illness for which we have no cure, as well as their families and loved ones. Help them to know that you claim them as your own, deliver them from fear and pain, and send your archangel Raphael to minister to their needs; for the sake of Jesus Christ, our Savior. *Amen.*

For Those Who are Unconscious

Merciful God, in your love and wisdom you know the needs and fears of your people before we can name them. Grant that N. and we who watch with *her/him* may be enabled to surrender all *her/his* cares to you, as you care for *her/him.* Give *her/him* peace of mind and unshakable trust in you; through Jesus Christ our Redeemer. *Amen.*

For the Dying

Blessed Jesus, in your last agony you commended your spirit to your Father. We seek your mercy for N., and all who are dying. May death become for them, as it was for you, a birth to everlasting life. Receive those whom we commend to you with the blessed assurance that whether we wake or sleep, we remain with you, one God, for ever. *Amen.*

For Those Who Mourn

Merciful God, whose Son Jesus wept at the death of Lazarus: look with compassion on all who are bound by sorrow and pain through the death of N. (*or* a loved one). Comfort them, grant them the conviction that all things work together for good to those who love you, and help them to find sure trust and confidence in your resurrection power; through Jesus Christ our deliverer. *Amen.*

For a Poor Prognosis

In your tender mercies O God, remember, N. who [*expects/has just received*] a grave diagnosis. Help *her/him* to trust in your goodness and believe that after a time of trial *she/he* shall be established on the firm foundation of your deliverance. *Amen.*

In the Evening

Keep watch, dear Lord, with those who work, or watch, or weep this night, and give your angels charge over those who sleep. Tend the sick, Lord Christ; give rest to the weary, bless the dying, soothe the suffering, pity the afflicted, shield the joyous; and all for your love's sake. *Amen.*

For a Person Who is Sick

God of all comfort, our very present help in trouble: be near to N. for whom our prayers are offered. Look on *her/him* with the eyes of your mercy; comfort *her/him* with a sense of your presence; preserve *her/him* from the enemy; and give *her/him* patience in *her/his* affliction. Restore *her/him* to health, and lead *her/him* to your eternal glory; through Jesus Christ our Lord. *Amen.*

For Protection

Christ, light of light, brightness indescribable, the Wisdom, power and glory of God, the Word made flesh: you overcame the forces of Satan, redeemed the world, then ascended again to the Father. Grant N., we pray, in this tarnished world, the shining of your splendor. Send your Archangel Michael to defend *her/him*, to guard *her/his* going out and coming in, and to bring *her/him* safely to your presence, where you reign in the one holy and undivided Trinity, to ages of ages. *Amen.*

For One Suffering from Mental Distress

Blessed Jesus, in the comfort of your love, we lay before you the memories that haunt N., the anxieties that perplex *her/him*, the despair that frightens *her/him*, and *her/his* frustration at *her/his* inability to think clearly. Help *her/him* to discover your forgiveness in *her/his* memories and know your peace in *her/his* distress. Touch *her/him*, O Lord, and fill *her/him* with your light and your hope. *Amen.*

For Recovery from Sickness

God, the strength of the weak and the comfort of those who suffer: Hear *our* prayers and grant N. the power of your grace, that *her/his* sickness may be turned into health, and *our* sorrow into joy; for Jesus Christ's sake. *Amen.*

or this

Spirit of all healing, visit your child N.; in your power, renew health within *her/him* and raise *her/him* up in joy, according to your loving-kindness, for which we give thanks and praise; through Jesus Christ our Savior. *Amen.*

For Strength and Confidence

Gracious God, only source of life and health: Help, comfort, and relieve [N.], and give your power of healing to those who minister to *her/his* needs; that *her/his* weakness may be turned to strength and confidence in your loving care; for the sake of Jesus Christ. *Amen.*

For the Sleepless

Holy and Blessed One, shine on *N.,* who lies sleepless. Illumine *her/his spirit* and give *her/him* rest in you, so that *she/he* may recognize you as the true God who brings us out of darkness into our eternal light. *Amen.*

For Rest

O God our refuge and strength: in this place of unrelenting light and noise, enfold *N.* in your holy darkness and silence, that *she/he* may rest secure under the shadow of your wings. *Amen.*

For the Sanctification of Illness

Sanctify, O Lord, the sickness of your servant *N.,* that the sense of *his* weakness may add strength to *his* faith and seriousness to *his* repentance; and grant that *he* may live with you in everlasting life; through Jesus Christ our Lord. *Amen.*

Before an Operation

Loving God, we pray that you will comfort *N.* in *her/his* suffering, lend skill to the hands of *her/his* healers, and bless the means used for *her/his* cure. Give *her/him* such confidence in the power of your grace, that even when *she/he* is afraid, *she/he* may put *her/his* whole trust in you; through our Savior Jesus Christ. *Amen.*

For an Extended Course of Treatment

Strengthen your servant *N.,* O God, to go where *she/he* has to go and bear what *she/he* has to bear; that, accepting your healing gifts at the hands of surgeons, nurses, and technicians, *she/he* may be restored to wholeness with a thankful heart; through Jesus Christ our Savior. *Amen.*

For Survivors of Abuse and Violence

Holy One, you do not distance yourself from the pain of your people, but in Jesus bear that pain with us and bless all who suffer at others' hands. Hallow our flesh and all creation; with your cleansing love bring healing and strength to *N.*; and by your justice, lift *her/him* up, that in the body you have given *her/him*, *she/he* may again rejoice. In Jesus' name we pray. *Amen.*

In Times of Personal Distress

Lord Christ, you came into the world as one of us, and suffered as we do. As we go through the trials of life, help us to realize that you are with us at all times and in all things; that we have no secrets from you; and that your loving grace enfolds us for eternity. In the security of your embrace we pray. *Amen.*

Thanksgiving for Recovery

God, your loving-kindness never fails, and your mercies are new every morning. We thank you for giving *N.* relief from pain and hope of health renewed. Continue the good work begun in *her/him*; that increasing daily in wholeness and strength, *she/he* may rejoice in your goodness and so order *her/his* life always to think and do that which pleases you; through Jesus Christ our Redeemer. *Amen.*

For Those Who Fear Losing Hope

Loving God, inspire by your Holy Spirit those who are afraid of losing hope, especially *N.* for whom we now pray. Give *her/him* a fresh vision of your love, that *she/he* may find again what *she/he* fears *she/he* has lost. Grant *her/him* your powerful deliverance; through the One who makes all things new, Jesus Christ our Redeemer. *Amen.*

For Those Who are Developmentally Disabled

Giver of all grace, we pray your peace, which passes all understanding, for those who are developmentally disabled. Grant that
they may always be sustained in love, their gifts honored, and
their difficulties understood, that none may add to their troubles.
We ask this in the name of the one who comforted those who
were troubled in mind, Jesus our Savior. *Amen.*

Prayers for Use by a Sick Person

Any of the following prayers may be adapted as needed.

For Trust in God

O God, the source of all health: So fill my heart with faith in your love, that with calm expectancy I may make room for your power to possess me, and gracefully accept your healing; through Jesus Christ our Lord. Amen.

In Pain

Lord Jesus Christ, by your patience in suffering you hallowed earthly pain and gave us the example of obedience to your Father's will: Be near me in my time of weakness and pain; sustain me by your grace, that my strength and courage may not fail; heal me according to you will; and help me always to believe that what happens to me here is of little account if you hold me in eternal life, my Lord and my God. Amen.

For Sleep

O heavenly Father, you give your children sleep for the refreshing of soul and body: Grant me this gift, I pray; keep me in that perfect peace which you have promised to those whose minds are fixed on you; and give me such a sense of your presence, that in the hours of silence I may enjoy the blessed assurance of your love; through Jesus Christ our Savior. Amen.

In the Morning

This is another day, O Lord. I know not what it will bring forth, but make me ready, Lord, for whatever it may be. If I am to stand up, help me to stand bravely. If I am to sit still, help me to sit quietly. If I am to lie low, help me to do it patiently. And if I am to do nothing, let me do it gallantly. Make these words more than words, and give me the Spirit of Jesus. Amen.

In the Evening

Keep watch, dear Lord, with those who work, or watch, or weep this night, and give your angels charge over those who sleep. Tend the sick, Lord Christ; give rest to the weary, bless the dying, soothe the suffering, pity the afflicted, shield the joyous; and all for your love's sake. Amen.

A Child's Prayer

Jesus, our Redeemer, Good Shepherd of the sheep, you carry the lambs in your arms. I place myself in your loving care. Stop my pain, give me help and strength, and raise me up to a life of joy. Hear me, I pray, for your dear Name's sake. Amen.

or this

Gentle Jesus, stay beside me through this day [night]. Take away my pain. Keep me safe. Help me in my fear. Make my body strong again and my heart glad. Thank you for your love which surrounds me always. Amen.

For a Sick Person

God of all comfort, our very present help in trouble, be near to me. Look on me with the eyes of your mercy; comfort me with a sense of your presence; preserve me from the enemy; and give me patience in my affliction. Restore me to health, and lead me to your eternal glory; through Jesus Christ our Lord. Amen.

For Protection

Christ, light of light, brightness indescribable, the Wisdom, power and glory of God, the Word made flesh: you overcame the forces of Satan, redeemed the world, then ascended again to the Father. Grant me, I pray, in this tarnished world, the shining of your splendor. Send your Archangel Michael to defend me, to guard my going out and coming in, and to bring me safely to your presence, where you reign in the one holy and undivided Trinity, to ages of ages. Amen.

For One Suffering from Mental Distress

Blessed Jesus, in the comfort of your love, I lay before you the memories that haunt me, the anxieties that perplex me, the despair that frightens me, and my frustration at my inability to think clearly. Help me to discover your forgiveness in my memories and know your peace in my distress. Touch me, O Lord, and fill me with your light and your hope. Amen.

For Recovery from Sickness

God, the strength of the weak and the comfort of those who suffer: Hear my prayers and grant me the power of your grace, that my sickness may be turned into health, and my sorrow into joy; for Jesus Christ's sake. Amen.

or this

Spirit of all healing, visit me, your child; in your power, renew health within me and raise me up in joy, according to your loving-kindness, for which I give thanks and praise; through Jesus Christ our Savior. Amen.

For Strength and Confidence

Gracious God, only source of life and health: Help, comfort, and relieve me, and give your power of healing to those who minister to my needs; that my weakness may be turned to strength and confidence in your loving care; for the sake of Jesus Christ. Amen.

For the Sleepless

Holy and Blessed One: shine on me as I lie sleepless. Illumine my spirit and give me rest in you, so that I may recognize you as the true God who brings us out of darkness into our eternal light. Amen.

For Rest

O God my refuge and strength: in this place of unrelenting light and noise, enfold me in your holy darkness and silence, that I may rest secure under the shadow of your wings. Amen.

For Sanctification of Illness

Sanctify, O Holy One, my sickness, that awareness of weakness may add strength to my faith and determination to my repentance; and grant that I may be made whole, according to your will; through Jesus Christ our Savior. Amen.

Before an Operation

Loving God, I pray that you will comfort me in my suffering, lend skill to the hands of my healers, and bless the means used for my cure. Give me such confidence in the power of your grace, that even when I am afraid, I may put my whole trust in you; through our Savior Jesus Christ. Amen.

or this

Keep me, Holy One, as the apple of your eye. Though I fear anesthesia, help me rest myself in your watchful care, and awake in the firm hope of your healing. Amen.

For an Extended Course of Treatment

Strengthen me, O God, to go where I have to go and bear what I have to bear; that, accepting your healing gifts at the hands of surgeons, nurses, and technicians, I may be restored to wholeness with a thankful heart; through Jesus Christ our Savior. Amen.

For Survivors of Abuse and Violence

Holy One, you do not distance yourself from the pain of your people, but in Jesus bear that pain with us and bless all who suffer at others' hands. Hallow my flesh and all creation; with your cleansing love bring me healing and strength; and by your justice, lift me up, that in the body you have given me, I may again rejoice. In Jesus' name I pray. Amen.

In Times of Personal Distress

Lord Christ, you came into the world as one of us, and suffered as we do. As I go through the trials of life, help me to realize that you are with me at all times and in all things; that I have no secrets from you; and that your loving grace enfolds me for eternity. In the security of your embrace I pray. Amen.

Thanksgiving for Recovery

God, your loving-kindness never fails and your mercies are new every morning. I thank you for giving me relief from pain and hope of health renewed. Continue the good work begun in me; that increasing daily in wholeness and strength, I may rejoice in your goodness and so order my life always to think and do that which pleases you; through Jesus Christ our Redeemer. Amen.

For One Who Fears Losing Hope

Loving God, by your Holy Spirit inspire me, as I fear losing hope. Give me a fresh vision of your love, that I may find again what I fear I have lost. Grant me your powerful deliverance; through the One who makes all things new, Jesus Christ our Redeemer. Amen.

For Those Who Are Developmentally Disabled

Giver of all grace, we pray your peace, which passes all understanding, for us who are developmentally disabled. Grant that we may always be sustained in love, our gifts honored, and our difficulties understood, that none may add to our troubles. We ask this in the name of the one who comforted those who were troubled in mind, Jesus our Savior. Amen.

In Thanksgiving

Thank you, Holy and Mighty One, for the many gifts of your love, even for the painful gift of fear which reminds me that only you are God. Into the mystery of your love I entrust myself. Dress me in the armor of your light and keep me safe; through Jesus Christ. Amen.

or this

In the midst of illness, God, I pause to give you thanks: for the glory of creation, which reveals in many forms your matchless beauty; for the life, death, and resurrection of Jesus our Savior; for your gift of my life and the presence of the Holy Spirit; for loved ones who care for me; and for the companionship of the Church. I thank you, blessed Trinity, holy God, for the gifts which sustain me in my time of need. Amen.

In Pain

As Jesus cried out on the cross, I cry out to you in pain, O God my Creator. Do not forsake me. Grant me relief from this suffering and preserve me in peace; through Jesus Christ my Savior, in the power of the Holy Spirit. Amen.

In Loss of Memory

Holy God, you have known me from my mother's womb, and have been with me throughout my life. Protect me and keep me safe through all the changes that may come. Since I am sealed as Christ's own, help me to trust that who I am will never be lost to you. Amen.

In Confinement

My Creator, you rolled out the heavens and spread the sky like a tent: bless to me the small confinement of this room, the long days, disturbances of night, immobility of body, and unease of soul, that this place of exile may become my holy ground, and Jesus my deliverer. Amen.

For Serenity

Merciful Jesus, you are my guide, the joy of my heart, the author of my hope, and the object of my love. I come seeking refreshment and peace. Show me your mercy, relieve my fears and anxieties, and grant me a quiet mind and an expectant heart, that by the assurance of your presence I may learn to abide in you, who is my Lord and my God. Amen.

or this

Jesus, let your mighty calmness lift me above my fears and frustrations. By your deep patience, give me tranquility and stillness of soul in you. Make me in this, and in all, more and more like you. Amen.

A Prayer of Thanksgiving for Caregivers

Merciful God, I thank you that since I have no strength to care for myself, you serve me through the hands and hearts of others. Bless these people that they may continue to serve you and please you all their days. Amen.

A Prayer of Comfort in God

God, you are my help and comfort; you shelter and surround me in love so tender that I may know your presence with me, now and always. Amen.

In Desolation

O God, why have you abandoned me? Though you have hidden your face from me, still from this dread and empty place, I cry to you, who have promised me that underneath are your everlasting arms. Amen.

After the Loss of a Pregnancy

O God, who gathered Rachel's tears over her lost children, hear now *my/our* sorrow and distress at the death of *my/our* expected child; in the darkness of loss, stretch out to *me/us* the strength of your arm and renewed assurance of your love; through your own suffering and risen Child Jesus. Amen.

or when appropriate

Holy God, I lament I have not had strength to hold, bear, and nurture the new life you have sent. Lift me up from my distress. Fill my grieving heart. Renew my hope. Receive the child I return to you into the arms of your mercy, for which I also yearn. Amen.

For Diagnosis of Terminal Illness

O God, only you number my days. Help me to look bravely at the end of my life in this world, while trusting in my life in the next. Journey with me toward my unexplored horizon where Jesus my Savior has gone before. Amen.

For Difficult Treatment Choices

Jesus, at Gethsemane you toiled with terrifying choices. Be with me now as I struggle with a fearful choice of treatments which promise much discomfort and offer no guarantee of long-term good. Help me know that you will bless my choice to me, and, good Savior, be my companion on the way. Amen.

In addition to the psalms listed above, the following may be helpful in times of distress:

Psalm 22

1 My God, my God, why have you forsaken me? *
    and are so far from my cry
    and from the words of my distress?

2 O my God, I cry in the daytime, but you do not answer; *
    by night as well, but I find no rest.

3 Yet you are the Holy One, *
    enthroned upon the praises of Israel.

4 Our forefathers put their trust in you; *
    they trusted, and you delivered them.

5 They cried out to you and were delivered; *
    they trusted in you and were not put to shame.

6 But as for me, I am a worm and no man, *
    scorned by all and despised by the people.

7 All who see me laugh me to scorn; *
    they curl their lips and wag their heads, saying,

8 "He trusted in the Lord; let him deliver him; *
    let him rescue him, if he delights in him."

9 Yet you are he who took me out of the womb, *
    and kept me safe upon my mother's breast.

10 I have been entrusted to you ever since I was born; *
    you were my God when I was still in my
        mother's womb.

11 Be not far from me, for trouble is near, *
    and there is none to help.

12 Many young bulls encircle me; *
    strong bulls of Bashan surround me.

13 They open wide their jaws at me, *
    like a ravening and a roaring lion.

14 I am poured out like water;
    all my bones are out of joint; *
    my heart within my breast is melting wax.

15 My mouth is dried out like a pot-sherd;
    my tongue sticks to the roof of my mouth; *
    and you have laid me in the dust of the grave.

16 Packs of dogs close me in,
    and gangs of evildoers circle around me; *
        they pierce my hands and my feet;
        I can count all my bones.

17 They stare and gloat over me; *
    they divide my garments among them;
    they cast lots for my clothing.

18 Be not far away, O LORD; *
    you are my strength; hasten to help me.

19 Save me from the sword, *
    my life from the power of the dog.

20 Save me from the lion's mouth, *
 my wretched body from the horns of wild bulls.

21 I will declare your Name to my brethren; *
 in the midst of the congregation I will praise you.

22 Praise the LORD, you that fear him; *
 stand in awe of him, O offspring of Israel;
 all you of Jacob's line, give glory

23 For he does not despise nor abhor the poor in their poverty;
 neither does he hide his face from them; *
 but when they cry to him he hears them.

24 My praise is of him in the great assembly; *
 I will perform my vows in the presence of those who
 worship him.

25 The poor shall eat and be satisfied,
 and those who seek the LORD shall praise him: *
 "May your heart live for ever!"

26 All the ends of the earth shall remember and turn to
 the Lord, *
 and all the families of the nations shall bow before him.

27 For kingship belongs to the LORD; *
 he rules over the nations.

28 To him alone all who sleep in the earth bow down
 in worship; *
 all who go down to the dust fall before him.

29 My soul shall live for him;
 my descendants shall serve him; *
 they shall be known as the LORD's for ever.

30 They shall come and make known to a people yet unborn *
    the saving deeds that he has done.

Psalm 25:15-21

15 Turn to me and have pity on me, *
    for I am left alone and in misery.

16 The sorrows of my heart have increased; *
    bring me out of my troubles.

17 Look upon my adversity and misery *
    and forgive me all my sin.

18 Look upon my enemies, for they are many, *
    and they bear a violent hatred against me.

19 Protect my life and deliver me; *
    let me not be put to shame, for I have trusted in you.

20 Let integrity and uprightness preserve me, *
    for my hope has been in you.

21 Deliver Israel, O God, *
    out of all his troubles.

Psalm 38

1 O LORD, do not rebuke me in your anger; *
    do not punish me in your wrath.

2 For your arrows have already pierced me, *
    and your hand presses hard upon me.

3 There is no health in my flesh,
    because of your indignation; *
        there is no soundness in my body, because of my sin.

4 For my iniquities overwhelm me; *
  like a heavy burden they are too much for me to bear.

5 My wounds stink and fester *
  by reason of my foolishness.

6 I am utterly bowed down and prostrate; *
  I go about in mourning all the day long.

7 My loins are filled with searing pain; *
  there is no health in my body.

8 I am utterly numb and crushed; *
  I wail, because of the groaning of my heart.

9 O Lord, you know all my desires, *
  and my sighing is not hidden from you.

10 My heart is pounding, my strength has failed me, *
  and the brightness of my eyes is gone from me.

11 My friends and companions draw back from my affliction; *
  my neighbors stand afar off.

12 Those who seek after my life lay snares for me; *
  those who strive to hurt me speak of my ruin
    and plot treachery all the day long.

13 But I am like the deaf who do not hear, *
  like those who are mute and do not open their mouth.

14 I have become like one who does not hear *
  and from whose mouth comes no defense.

15 For in you, O LORD, have I fixed my hope; *
  you will answer me, O Lord my God.

16 For I said, "Do not let them rejoice at my expense, *
  those who gloat over me when my foot slips."

17 Truly, I am on the verge of falling, *
  and my pain is always with me.

18 I will confess my iniquity *
  and be sorry for my sin.

19 Those who are my enemies without cause are mighty, *
  and many in number are those who wrongfully hate me.

20 Those who repay evil for good slander me, *
  because I follow the course that is right.

21 O LORD, do not forsake me; *
  be not far from me, O my God.

22 Make haste to help me, *
  O LORD of my salvation.

Psalm 46

1 God is our refuge and strength, *
  a very present help in trouble.

2 Therefore we will not fear, though the earth be moved, *
  and though the mountains be toppled into the
  depths of the sea;

3 Though its waters rage and foam, *
  and though the mountains tremble at its tumult.

4 The LORD of hosts is with us; *
  the God of Jacob is our stronghold.

5 There is a river whose streams make glad the city of God, *
    the holy habitation of the Most High.

6 God is in the midst of her;
  she shall not be overthrown; *
    God shall help her at the break of day.

7 The nations make much ado, and the kingdoms are shaken; *
    God has spoken, and the earth shall melt away.

8 The LORD of hosts is with us; *
    the God of Jacob is our stronghold.

9 Come now and look upon the works of the LORD, *
    what awesome things he has done on earth.

10 It is he who makes war to cease in all the world; *
  he breaks the bow, and shatters the spear,
    and burns the shields with fire.

11 "Be still, then, and know that I am God; *
  I will be exalted among the nations;
    I will be exalted in the earth."

12 The LORD of hosts is with us; *
    the God of Jacob is our stronghold.

Psalm 69:31-38

31 As for me, I am afflicted and in pain; *
    your help, O God, will lift me up on high.

32 I will praise the Name of God in song; *
    I will proclaim his greatness with thanksgiving.

33 This will please the Lord more than an offering of oxen, *
    more than bullocks with horns and hoofs.

34 The afflicted shall see and be glad; *
    you who seek God, your heart shall live.

35 For the Lord listens to the needy, *
    and his prisoners he does not despise.

36 Let the heavens and the earth praise him, *
    the seas and all that moves in them;

37 For God will save Zion and rebuild the cities of Judah; *
    they shall live there and have it in possession.

38 The children of his servants will inherit it, *
    and those who love his Name will dwell therein.

Psalm 88

1 O LORD, my God, my Savior, *
    by day and night I cry to you.

2 Let my prayer enter into your presence; *
    incline your ear to my lamentation.

3 For I am full of trouble; *
    my life is at the brink of the grave.

4 I am counted among those who go down to the Pit; *
    I have become like one who has no strength;

5 Lost among the dead, *
    like the slain who lie in the grave,

6 Whom you remember no more, *
    for they are cut off from your hand.

7 You have laid me in the depths of the Pit, *
    in dark places, and in the abyss.

8 Your anger weighs upon me heavily, *
    and all your great waves overwhelm me.

9 You have put my friends far from me;
    you have made me to be abhorred by them; *
      I am in prison and cannot get free.

10 My sight has failed me because of trouble; *
    LORD, I have called upon you daily;
    I have stretched out my hands to you.

11 Do you work wonders for the dead? *
    will those who have died stand up and give you thanks?

12 Will your loving-kindness be declared in the grave? *
    your faithfulness in the land of destruction?

13 Will your wonders be known in the dark? *
    or your righteousness in the country where all
      is forgotten?

14 But as for me, O LORD, I cry to you for help; *
    in the morning my prayer comes before you.

15 LORD, why have you rejected me? *
    why have you hidden your face from me?

16 Ever since my youth, I have been wretched and at the
      point of death; *
    I have borne your terrors with a troubled mind.

17 Your blazing anger has swept over me; *
    your terrors have destroyed me;

18 They surround me all day long like a flood; *
    they encompass me on every side.

19 My friend and my neighbor you have put away from me, *
    and darkness is my only companion.

Psalm 116

1 I love the LORD, because he has heard the voice of
        my supplication, *
  because he has inclined his ear to me whenever
        I called upon him.

2 The cords of death entangled me;
  the grip of the grave took hold of me; *
    I came to grief and sorrow.

3 Then I called upon the Name of the LORD: *
    "O LORD, I pray you, save my life."

4 Gracious is the LORD and righteous; *
    our God is full of compassion.

5 The LORD watches over the innocent; *
    I was brought very low, and he helped me.

6 Turn again to your rest, O my soul, *
    for the LORD has treated you well.

7 For you have rescued my life from death, *
    my eyes from tears, and my feet from stumbling.

8 I will walk in the presence of the LORD *
    in the land of the living.

9 I believed, even when I said,
  "I have been brought very low." *
    In my distress I said, "No one can be trusted."

10 How shall I repay the LORD *
    for all the good things he has done for me?

11 I will lift up the cup of salvation *
    and call upon the Name of the LORD.

12 I will fulfill my vows to the LORD *
    in the presence of all his people.

13 Precious in the sight of the LORD *
    is the death of his servants.

14 O LORD, I am your servant; *
    I am your servant and the child of your handmaid;
    you have freed me from my bonds.

15 I will offer you the sacrifice of thanksgiving *
    and call upon the Name of the LORD.

16 I will fulfill my vows to the LORD *
    in the presence of all his people,

17 In the courts of the LORD's house, *
    in the midst of you, O Jerusalem.
    Hallelujah!

Psalm 121

1 I lift up my eyes to the hills; *
    from where is my help to come?

2 My help comes from the LORD, *
    the maker of heaven and earth.

3 He will not let your foot be moved *
    and he who watches over you will not fall asleep.

4 Behold, he who keeps watch over Israel *
    shall neither slumber nor sleep;

5 The LORD himself watches over you; *
   the LORD is your shade at your right hand,

6 So that the sun shall not strike you by day, *
   nor the moon by night.

7 The LORD shall preserve you from all evil; *
   it is he who shall keep you safe.

8 The LORD shall watch over your going out and
         your coming in, *
   from this time forth for evermore.

Psalm 130

1 Out of the depths have I called to you, O LORD;
   LORD, hear my voice; *
      let your ears consider well the voice of my supplication.

2 If you, LORD, were to note what is done amiss, *
   O Lord, who could stand?

3 For there is forgiveness with you; *
   therefore you shall be feared.

4 I wait for the LORD; my soul waits for him; *
   in his word is my hope.

5 My soul waits for the LORD,
   more than watchmen for the morning, *
      more than watchmen for the morning.

6 O Israel, wait for the LORD, *
   for with the LORD there is mercy;

7 With him there is plenteous redemption, *
   and he shall redeem Israel from all their sins.

Canticle I

A Song of Jonah
Jonah 2:2-7, 9

I called to you, O God, out of my distress, and you answered me; *
   out of the belly of Sheol I cried, and you heard my voice.
You cast me into the deep, into the heart of the seas, *
   and the flood surrounded me;
   all your waves and billows passed over me.
Then I said, "I am driven away from your sight; *
   how shall I ever look again upon your holy temple?"
The waters closed in over me, the deep was round about me; *
   weeds were wrapped around my head at the roots
     of the mountains.
I went down to the land beneath the earth, *
   yet you brought up my life from the depths, O God.
As my life was ebbing away, I remembered you, O God, *
   and my prayer came to you, into your holy temple.
With the voice of thanksgiving, I will sacrifice to you; *
   what I have vowed I will pay, for deliverance belongs to the Lord!

Canticle Q

A Song of Christ's Goodness
Anselm of Canterbury

Jesus, as a mother you gather your people to you; *
   you are gentle with us as a mother with her children.
Often you weep over our sins and our pride, *
   tenderly you draw us from hatred and judgment.
You comfort us in sorrow and bind up our wounds, *
   in sickness you nurse us and with pure milk you feed us.
Jesus, by your dying, we are born to new life; *
   by your anguish and labor we come forth in joy.

Despair turns to hope through your sweet goodness; *
   through your gentleness, we find comfort in fear.
Your warmth gives life to the dead, *
   your touch makes sinners righteous.
Lord Jesus, in your mercy, heal us; *
   in your love and tenderness, remake us.
In your compassion, bring grace and forgiveness, *
   for the beauty of heaven, may your love prepare us.

Canticle R

A Song of the True Motherhood
Julian of Norwich

God chose to be our mother in all things *
   and so made the foundation of his work,
   most humbly and most pure, in the Virgin's womb.
God, the perfect wisdom of all, *
   arrayed himself in this humble place.
Christ came in our poor flesh *
   to share a mother's care.
Our mothers bear us for pain and for death; *
   our true mother, Jesus, bears us for joy and endless life.
Christ carried us within him in love and travail, *
   until the full time of his passion.
And when all was completed and he had carried us so for joy, *
   still all this could not satisfy the power of his wonderful love.
All that we owe is redeemed in truly loving God, *
   for the love of Christ works in us;
Christ is the one whom we love.

Additional Prayers

Any of the following prayers may be adapted as needed.

For Caregivers and Others in Support of the Sick

Lover of souls, we bless your Holy Name for all who are called to mediate your grace to those who are sick or infirm. Sustain them by your Holy Spirit, that they may bring your loving-kindness to those in pain, fear, and confusion; that in bearing one another's burdens they may follow the example of our Savior Jesus Christ. *Amen.*

or this

Compassionate God, support and strengthen all those who reach out in love, concern, and prayer for the sick and distressed. In their acts of compassion, may they know that they are your instruments. In their concerns and fears may they know your peace. In their prayer may they know your steadfast love. May they not grow weary or faint-hearted, for your mercy's sake. *Amen.*

For Companions to Those Who Are Chronically Ill

O God, surround N. [*and N.*] with your compassion as *she/he/they* live[s] with N. in sickness. Help N. [*and N.*] to accept the limits of what *she/he/they* can do, that feelings of helplessness and frustration [and anger] may be transformed into serene acceptance and joyful hope in you. Let *her/him/them* remember the grief and love of Jesus over the afflictions of his friends, knowing that God too weeps. Bring *her/him/them* gladness and strengthened love in *her/his/their* service; through Christ our companion. *Amen.*

At the Limits of Our Power to Help

O Lord, we are at the limits of our power to help. For what we have left undone, forgive us. For what you have helped us to do, we thank you. For what must be done by others, lend your strength. Now shelter us in your peace which passes our understanding. *Amen.*

For Those Who Are Sick and Those Who Minister to Them

Gracious God, source of life and health: Jesus came to our disordered world to make your people whole. Send your Spirit on those who are sick and all who minister to them; that when the sick enter your peace, they may offer thanks to your Great Name; through Jesus Christ our Savior. *Amen.*

For Health Care Providers

Give your blessing, gracious God, to those whom you have called to the study and practice of the arts of healing, and the prevention of disease and pain. Give them the wisdom of your Holy Spirit, that through their work the health of our community may be advanced and your creation glorified; through your Son Jesus Christ. *Amen.*

For Emergency Workers

God our strong deliverer: when those charged with the urgent mediation of your healing power feel overwhelmed by the numbers of the suffering, uphold them in their fatigue and banish their despair. Let them see with your eyes, so they may know all their patients as precious. Give comfort, and renew their energy and compassion, for the sake of Jesus in whom is our life and our hope. *Amen.*

or this

Divine Physician, hear our prayers for those in emergency medicine. By your healing power, grant them quick minds and skillful hands. Strengthen them in times of trauma. In quiet times, give them rest and assurance of the value of their work. Keep them ever prepared for the work you have called them to do, for your mercy's sake. *Amen.*

For Relatives of an Organ Donor

Blessed Jesus, who said "unless a grain of wheat falls to the earth and dies, it shall not live," help us to release N. to everlasting life, and N.'s body to give new life to others you also love, as you have given your body that we might have life abundant, for which we give great thanks. *Amen.*

Ministration at the Time of Death

When a person is near death, the member of the clergy in charge of the congregation should be notified, so that the ministrations of the Church may be provided. A person approaching death may be offered an opportunity for the Reconciliation of a Penitent.

The rite which follows may be shortened or extended as seems appropriate, and the prayers may be adapted as needed.

The minister greets those present in these or similar words

In the name of God, the holy and undivided Trinity. *Amen.*

or this

In the Name of the Father, and of the Son, and of the Holy Spirit. *Amen.*

The minister continues

Let us pray.

Gracious God, lover of souls, look on *N.*, lying in great weakness, and comfort *him/her* with the promise of everlasting life, given in the resurrection of your Son Jesus Christ our Savior. *Amen.*

or this

Christ our Redeemer, deliver *N.* from all evil and the power of death, that *he/she* may rest with all your saints in the eternal habitations; where with the Father and the Holy Spirit you live and reign, one God, for ever and ever. *Amen.*

or this—for a sudden death

O God our strength in need, our help in trouble: stand with us in our distress, support us in our shock, bless us in our questioning, and do not leave us comfortless, but raise us up with Jesus Christ. *Amen.*

or this—for a death by violence

O God our Vindicator, come speedily to our help. Receive the soul of *N.*, your child, into the arms of your mercy, and deliver *his/her* assailant to justice, that your holy Law may be served, and your peace renewed; through Jesus our Savior. *Amen.*

or this—for the death of a very young child

God our Creator, you called into being this fragile life, which had seemed to us so full of promise: give to *N.*, whom we commit to your care, abundant life in your presence, and to us who grieve for hopes destroyed, courage to bear our loss; through Jesus Christ our Savior. *Amen.*

or this—for the death of a child

God, as Mary stood at the foot of the cross, we come before you with broken hearts and tearful eyes. Keep us mindful that you know our pain, and free us to see your resurrection power already at work in *N.'s* life. In your time, raise us from our grief as you are raising *N.* to eternal life; through Jesus Christ our Savior. *Amen.*

One of the following or some other Psalm may be said

Psalm 23

1 The LORD is my shepherd;*
    I shall not be in want.

2 He makes me lie down in green pastures*
    and leads me beside still waters.

3 He revives my soul*
    and guides me along right pathways for his Name's sake.

4 Though I walk through the valley of the shadow of death,
    I shall fear no evil;*
        for you are with me;
        your rod and your staff, they comfort me.

5 You spread a table before me in the presence of those who
    trouble me;*
        you have anointed my head with oil,
        and my cup is running over.

6 Surely your goodness and mercy shall follow me all the days
    of my life,*
        and I will dwell in the house of the LORD for ever.

Psalm 61:1-5

1 Hear my cry, O God,*
    and listen to my prayer.

2 I call upon you from the ends of the earth
    with heaviness in my heart;*
        set me upon the rock that is higher than I.

3 For you have been my refuge,*
    a strong tower against the enemy.

4 I will dwell in your house for ever;*
      I will take refuge under the cover of your wings.

5 For you, O God, have heard my vows;*
      you have granted me the heritage of those who fear your Name.

Psalm 121

1 I will lift up my eyes to the hills;*
      from where is my help to come?

2 My help comes from the LORD,*
      the maker of heaven and earth.

3 He will not let your foot be moved*
      and he who watches over you will not fall asleep.

4 Behold, he who keeps watch over Israel*
      shall neither slumber nor sleep;

5 The LORD himself watches over you;*
      the LORD is your shade at your right hand,

6 So that the sun shall not strike you by day,*
      nor the moon by night.

7 The LORD shall preserve you from all evil;*
      it is he who shall keep you safe.

8 The LORD shall watch over your going out and your coming in,*
      from this time forth for evermore.

Psalm 130

1 Out of the depths have I called to you, O LORD;
   LORD, hear my voice;*
      let your ears consider well the voice of my supplication.

2 If you, LORD, were to note what is done amiss,*
 O Lord, who could stand?

3 For there is forgiveness with you;*
 therefore you shall be feared.

4 I wait for the LORD; my soul waits for him;*
 in his word is my hope.

5 My soul waits for the LORD,
more than watchmen for the morning,*
 more than watchmen for the morning.

6 O Israel, wait for the LORD,*
 for with the LORD there is mercy;

7 With him there is plenteous redemption,*
 and he shall redeem Israel from all their sins.

Psalm 139:1-17

1 LORD, you have searched me out and known me; *
 you know my sitting down and my rising up;
 you discern my thoughts from afar.

2 You trace my journeys and my resting-places *
 and are acquainted with all my ways.

3 Indeed, there is not a word on my lips, *
 but you, O LORD, know it altogether.

4 You press upon me behind and before *
 and lay your hand upon me.

5 Such knowledge is too wonderful for me; *
 it is so high that I cannot attain to it.

6 Where can I go then from your Spirit? *
   where can I flee from your presence?

7 If I climb up to heaven, you are there; *
   if I make the grave my bed, you are there also.

8 If I take the wings of the morning *
   and dwell in the uttermost parts of the sea,

9 Even there your hand will lead me *
   and your right hand hold me fast.

10 If I say, "Surely the darkness will cover me, *
   and the light around me turn to night,"

11 Darkness is not dark to you;
   the night is as bright as the day; *
      darkness and light to you are both alike.

12 For you yourself created my inmost parts; *
   you knit me together in my mother's womb.

13 I will thank you because I am marvelously made; *
   your works are wonderful, and I know it well.

14 My body was not hidden from you, *
   while I was being made in secret
   and woven in the depths of the earth.

15 Your eyes beheld my limbs, yet unfinished in the womb;
   all of them were written in your book; *
      they were fashioned day by day,
      when as yet there was none of them.

16 How deep I find your thoughts, O God! *
   how great is the sum of them!

17 If I were to count them, they would be more in number
     than the sand; *
     to count them all, my life span would need to be like yours.

Litany at the Time of Death

The minister invites those gathered into prayer, using these or similar words

Let us offer our prayers for N., saying, "We commend N. to you."

Holy God, Creator of heaven and earth,
We commend N. to you.

Holy and Mighty, Redeemer of the world,
We commend N. to you.

Holy Immortal One, Sanctifier of the faithful,
We commend N. to you.

Holy, blessed and glorious Trinity, one God,
We commend N. to you.

By your Holy Incarnation,
We commend N. to you.

By your Cross and Passion,
We commend N. to you.

By your precious death and burial,
We commend N. to you.

By your glorious Resurrection and Ascension,
We commend N. to you.

By the coming of the Holy Spirit,
We commend N. *to you.*

For deliverance from all evil, all sin, and all tribulation,
We commend N. *to you.*

For deliverance from eternal death,
We commend N. *to you.*

For forgiveness of all sins,
We commend N. *to you.*

For a place of refreshment at your heavenly banquet,
We commend N. *to you.*

For joy and gladness with your saints in light,
We commend N. *to you.*

Jesus, Lamb of God:
We commend N. *to you.*

Jesus, bearer of our sins:
We commend N. *to you.*

Jesus, redeemer of the world:
We commend N. *to you.*

As our Savior Christ
has taught us,
we now pray,

And now, as our Savior
Christ has taught us,
we are bold to say,

Officiant and People

Officiant and People

Our Father in heaven,
   hallowed be your Name,
   your kingdom come,
   your will be done,
     on earth as in heaven.
Give us today our daily bread.
Forgive us our sins
   as we forgive those
   who sin against us.
Save us from the time of trial,
   and deliver us from evil.
For the kingdom, the power,
   and the glory are yours,
   now and for ever. Amen.

Our Father, who art in heaven,
   hallowed be thy Name,
   thy kingdom come,
   thy will be done,
     on earth as it is in heaven.
Give us this day our daily bread.
And forgive us our trespasses,
   as we forgive those
   who trespass against us.
And lead us not into temptation,
   but deliver us from evil.
For thine is the kingdom,
   and the power, and the glory
   for ever and ever. Amen.

or this

Litany at the Time of Death

God the Father,
Have mercy on your servant.

God the Son,
Have mercy on your servant.

God the Holy Spirit,
Have mercy on your servant.

Holy Trinity, one God,
Have mercy on your servant.

From all evil, from all sin, from all tribulation,
Good Lord, deliver him.

By your holy Incarnation, by your Cross and Passion, by your precious Death and Burial,
Good Lord, deliver him.

By your glorious Resurrection and Ascension, and by the Coming of the Holy Spirit,
Good Lord, deliver him.

We sinners beseech you to hear us, Lord Christ: That it may please you to deliver the soul of your servant from the power of evil, and from eternal death,
We beseech you to hear us, good Lord.

That it may please you mercifully to pardon all *his* sins.
We beseech you to hear us, good Lord.

That it may please you to grant *him* a place of refreshment and everlasting blessedness,
We beseech you to hear us, good Lord.

That it may please you to give *him* joy and gladness in your kingdom, with your saints in light,
We beseech you to hear us, good Lord.

Jesus, Lamb of God:
Have mercy on him.

Jesus, bearer of our sins:
Have mercy on him.

Jesus, redeemer of the world:
Give him *your peace.*

Lord, have mercy.
Christ, have mercy.
Lord, have mercy.

Officiant and People

Our Father in heaven,
   hallowed be your Name,
   your kingdom come,
   your will be done,
     on earth as in heaven.
Give us today our daily bread.
Forgive us our sins
   as we forgive those
   who sin against us.
Save us from the time of trial,
   and deliver us from evil.
For the kingdom, the power,
   and the glory are yours,
   now and for ever. Amen.

Our Father, who art in heaven,
   hallowed be thy Name,
   thy kingdom come,
   thy will be done,
     on earth as it is in heaven.
Give us this day our daily bread.
And forgive us our trespasses,
   as we forgive those
   who trespass against us.
And lead us not into temptation,
   but deliver us from evil.
For thine is the kingdom,
   and the power, and the glory
   for ever and ever. Amen.

The Officiant says this Collect

Let us pray.

Deliver your servant, N., O Sovereign Lord Christ, from all evil, and set *him* free from every bond; that *he* may rest with all your saints in the eternal habitations; where with the Father and the Holy Spirit you live and reign, one God, for ever and ever. *Amen.*

Laying on of Hands [and Anointing]

Laying on of hands [and anointing] may be administered, using these or similar words

N., I lay my hands upon you [and anoint you] in the name of our Savior Jesus Christ. *Amen.*

Holy Communion

Communion from the reserved Sacrament may be administered with the following or other words

The Body and Blood of our Lord Jesus Christ keep you in everlasting life. [*Amen.*]

If the person cannot receive both the consecrated Bread and the Wine, it is suitable to administer the Sacrament in one kind only.

If the person is unable to eat and drink the Bread and Wine, the minister may pray, using these or similar words

Faithful God,
in the wonder of your wisdom and love
you fed your people in the wilderness with the bread of angels,
and you sent Jesus to be the bread of life.
Though N. cannot consume these gifts of Bread and Wine,
we thank you that *he/she* has received the sacrament of Christ's presence,
the forgiveness of sins, and all other benefits of Christ's passion.
By the power of the Holy Spirit,
may we embody your desire
and be renewed for your service
through Jesus Christ our Savior. *Amen.*

or this

God of infinite mercy,
we thank you for Jesus our Savior, our true Mother
who feeds us and gives us eternal life.
Though N. cannot consume these gifts of Bread and Wine,
we thank you that *he/she* has received the sacrament of Christ's presence,
the forgiveness of sins, and all other benefits of Christ's passion.
Grant that we may continue for ever in the Risen Life of our Savior,
who with you and the Holy Spirit,
lives and reigns, one God, now and for ever. *Amen.*

Concluding Collects

The minister may pray

Lord Jesus Christ, Son of the living God, we pray you to set your passion, cross, and death between your judgment and our souls, now and in the hour of our death. Give mercy and grace to the living; pardon and rest to the dead; to your holy Church peace and concord; and to us sinners everlasting life and glory; for with the Father and Holy Spirit you live and reign, one God, now and for ever. *Amen.*

or this

God of mercy, look kindly on N. as death comes near. Release *him/her*, and set *him/her* free by your grace to enter into the company of the saints in light. Be with us as we watch and wait, and keep us in the assurance of your love; through Jesus Christ. *Amen.*

Commendation at the Time of Death

The minister may introduce the commendation in these or similar words

Let us commend our *brother/sister* N. to the mercy of God, our Maker and Redeemer.

The minister continues

Savior, this soul is yours, sealed by your name, redeemed by your love: now released by the saints on earth to the glad companionship of the saints above, into your arms of mercy, into the blessed country of light.

May *his/her* soul and the souls of all who have died through your mercy rest in peace. *Amen.*

or this

N., our companion in faith and *brother/sister* in Christ,
   we entrust you to God.
Go forth from this world:
in the love of God who created you;
in the mercy of Jesus Christ who died for you;
in the power of the Holy Spirit who strengthens you,
at one with all the faithful, living and departed.
May you rest in peace and rise in the glory of your eternal home,
where grief and misery are banished, and light and joy abide.
Amen.

or this

Depart, O Christian soul, out of this world;
In the name of God the Father Almighty who created you;
In the name of Jesus Christ who redeemed you;
In the name of the Holy Spirit who sanctifies you.
May your rest be this day in peace,
   and your dwelling place in the Paradise of God.

or this

Merciful Savior, we commend to you our *brother/sister* N. Acknowledge, we pray, a sheep of your own fold, a lamb of your own flock, a sinner of your own redeeming. Receive *him/her* into the arms of your mercy, into the blessed rest of everlasting peace, and into the glorious company of the saints in light.

May *his/her* soul, and the souls of all the departed, through the mercy of God, rest in peace. *Amen.*

Additional Prayers

Almighty God, whose most dear Son went not up to joy but first he suffered pain, and entered not into glory before he was crucified: Mercifully grant that we, walking in the way of the cross, may find it none other than the way of life and peace; through Jesus Christ your Son our Lord, who lives and reigns with you and the Holy Spirit, one God, for ever and ever. *Amen.*

O God, who by the glorious resurrection of your Son Jesus Christ destroyed death and brought life and immortality to light: Grant that we, who have been raised with him, may abide in his presence and rejoice in the hope of eternal glory; through Jesus Christ our Lord, to whom, with you and the Holy Spirit, be dominion and praise for ever and ever. *Amen.*

O Lord, support us all the day long, until the shadows lengthen, and the evening comes, and the busy world is hushed, and the fever of life is over, and our work is done. In your mercy, grant us a safe lodging, and a holy rest, and peace at the last. *Amen.*

Gracious God, you sent Jesus into the world to bear our infirmities and endure our suffering: Look with compassion on N. Support *him/her* with your grace, comfort *him/her* with your protection, and give *him/her* victory over evil, sin, and death. Since [in Baptism] you have given N. a share in the passion of Christ, fulfill in *him/her* also the hope and expectation promised in the resurrection, through Christ, who with you and the Holy Spirit lives and reigns, one God, now and for ever. *Amen.*

For Release

Blessed Jesus, Living Water, Solid Rock: Uphold your child N.; loose the fetters of sickness, break *her/his* yoke of pain, and from this land of affliction, lead *her/him* home. *Amen.*

or this

God of life, you sent Jesus our Redeemer to your people so that we might be led triumphant through death's overwhelming flood into your radiant presence. In the waters of Baptism, N. was marked as your own for ever. Hold *him/her* now with mighty hand and outstretched arm as *he/she* crosses form death to life. Sustain *him/her* with a sure and certain hope of the resurrection, and bring *him/her* into eternal glory. *Amen.*

For Those Who Mourn

Merciful God, whose Son Jesus wept at the death of Lazarus: look with compassion on all who are bound by sorrow and pain through the death of N., a loved one. Comfort them, grant them the conviction that all things work together for good to those who love you, and help them to find sure trust and confidence in your resurrection power; through Jesus Christ our deliverer. *Amen.*

A Litany Anticipating Heaven

This litany is also appropriate for use when the body is removed from the home or other place of death.

The minister invites the people to pray in these or similar words

Let us pray with confidence, anticipating heaven, and let the people respond, "Lead your child home."

The minister continues

To the gates of Paradise
Lead your child home.

To your mercy-seat
Lead your child home.

To the kingdom of heaven
Lead your child home.

To your true sanctuary
Lead your child home.

To the multitude of the blessed
Lead your child home.

To the welcome-table
Lead your child home.

To the nuptial chamber
Lead your child home.

To the New Jerusalem
Lead your child home.

To eternal bliss
Lead your child home.

To the company of the saints
Lead your child home.

To the Supper of the Lamb
Lead your child home.

To the garden of delight
Lead your child home.

To the throne of majesty
Lead your child home.

To the lights of glory
Lead your child home.

To the Canaan-ground
Lead your child home.

To the highest heights
Lead your child home.

To the crown of glory
Lead your child home.

To the land of rest
Lead your child home.

To Jordan's other shore
Lead your child home.

To the Holy City, the Bride
Lead your child home.

To the safe harbor
Lead your child home.

To the fount of life
Lead your child home.

To the gates of pearl
Lead your child home.

To the ladder of angels
Lead your child home.

To the land of milk and honey
Lead your child home.

To the clouds of glory
Lead your child home.

To the refreshing stream
Lead your child home.

To the reward of the righteous
Lead your child home.

To the dwelling-place of God
Lead your child home.

Additional Psalms

Psalm 71

1 In you, O LORD, have I taken refuge;*
   let me never be ashamed.

2 In your righteousness, deliver me and set me free;*
   incline your ear to me and save me.

3 Be my strong rock, a castle to keep me safe;*
   you are my crag and my stronghold.

4 Deliver me, my God, from the hand of the wicked,*
   from the clutches of the evildoer and the oppressor.

5 For you are my hope, O Lord GOD,*
   my confidence since I was young.

6 I have been sustained by you ever since I was born;
   from my mother's womb you have been my strength;*
   my praise shall be always of you.

7 I have become a portent to many;*
   but you are my refuge and my strength.

8 Let my mouth be full of your praise*
   and your glory all the day long.

9 Do not cast me off in my old age;*
   forsake me not when my strength fails.

10 For my enemies are talking against me,*
   and those who lie in wait for my life take counsel together.

11 They say, "God has forsaken him;
   go after him and seize him;*
   because there is none who will save."

12 O God, be not far from me;*
   come quickly to help me, O My God.

13 Let those who set themselves against me be put to shame
         and be disgraced;*
   let those who seek to do me evil be covered with scorn
         and reproach.

14 But I shall always wait in patience,*
   and shall praise you more and more.

15 My mouth shall recount your mighty acts and saving deeds
         all day long;*
   though I cannot know the number of them.

16 I will begin with the mighty works of the Lord GOD;*
   I will recall your righteousness, yours alone.

17 O God, you have taught me since I was young,*
   and to this day I tell of your wonderful works.

18 And now that I am old and gray-headed, O God, do not
         forsake me,*
   till I make known your strength to this generation
   and your power to all who are to come.

19 Your righteousness, O God, reaches to the heavens;*
   you have done great things; who is like you, O God?

20 You have showed me great troubles and adversities,*
   but you will restore my life
   and bring me up again from the deep places of the earth.

21 You strengthen me more and more;*
   you enfold and comfort me,

22 Therefore I will praise you upon the lyre for your
         faithfulness, O my God;*
   I will sing to you with the harp; O Holy One of Israel.

23 My lips will sing with joy when I play to you,*
   and so will my soul, which you have redeemed.

24 My tongue will proclaim your righteousness all day long,*
   for they are ashamed and disgraced who sought
       to do me harm.

Psalm 130

1 Out of the depths have I called to you, O LORD;
LORD, hear my voice;*
   let your ears consider well the voice of my supplication.

2 If you, LORD, were to note what is done amiss,*
   O Lord, who could stand?

3 For there is forgiveness with you;*
   therefore you shall be feared.

4 I wait for the LORD; my soul waits for him;*
   in his word is my hope.

5 My soul waits for the LORD,
more than watchmen for the morning,*
   more than watchmen for the morning.

6 O Israel, wait for the LORD,*
   for with the LORD there is mercy;

7 With him there is plenteous redemption,*
   and he shall redeem Israel from all their sins.

A Form of Prayer
When Life-Sustaining Treatment
Is Withheld or Discontinued

This rite is appropriate when family, friends, and/or caregivers gather for prayer to mark a transition from life-sustaining to palliative care. It may also be used when extraordinary measures are to be withheld or discontinued.

The service is appropriate for situations in which death is expected to follow not long after the withholding or discontinuing of treatment. When death is expected immediately after the withholding or discontinuing of treatment, traditional rites at time of death might be preferred.

The service may be abbreviated or lengthened as needed.

The minister may begin the service with the following sentence

The Lamb at the center of the throne will be their shepherd, and he will guide them to springs of the water of life, and God will wipe away every tear from their eyes.
Revelation 7:17

The minister continues

Let us pray.

O God our Creator and Sustainer, receive our prayers for N. We thank you for the love and companionship we have shared with *him/her.* Give us grace now to accept the limits of human healing as we commend N. to your merciful care. Strengthen us, we pray, in this time of trial and help us to continue to serve and care for one another; through Jesus Christ our Savior. *Amen.*

In a Time of Difficult Decision

Lord of all wisdom and source of all life, we come before you as we struggle with decisions about life and death that rightly belong to you alone. We confess that we act with uncertainty now. Give us your help, and guide us, merciful God, in your loving concern for *N.* who lies in grave illness; through Jesus Christ our Redeemer. *Amen.*

One or more of the following passages of scripture may be read.

From the Old Testament

Isaiah 49:14-16a (I will not forget you)
Isaiah 65:17-20 (I am about to create new heavens and a new earth)

Psalms 23; 103

From the New Testament

Romans 6:3-4, 8-11 (death no longer has dominion)
Romans 8:35, 38-39 (Who will separate us from the love of Christ?)
1 Corinthians 15:51-58 (I will tell you a mystery!)

The Gospel

John 14:1-3 (In my father's house)

One or both of the following litanies may be prayed.

A Litany for the Discontinuing of Life-Sustaining Treatment: Form 1

The Minister introduces the litany with these or similar words

Let us pray to God, the helper and lover of souls, saying "Holy One, help us!"

That we may know your near presence with us, blessed God:
Holy One, help us!

That N. may be released from the bondage of suffering, blessed God:
Holy One, help us!

That our actions may proceed from love, blessed God:
Holy One, help us!

That our best judgments may accord with your will, blessed God:
Holy One, help us!

That you will hold N. and us in the palm of your hand this day,
blessed God:
Holy One, help us!

That all our fears may be relieved as we place our trust in you,
blessed God:
Holy One, help us!

That as N. labors into new resurrection birth, we may surround
him/her with courage, blessed God:
Holy One, help us!

That although we now grieve, joy may return in the morning,
blessed God:
Holy One, help us!

The Minister adds the following or some other Collect

God our Wisdom: Bless the decisions we have made in hope, in
sorrow, and in love; that as we place our whole trust in you, our
choices and our actions may be encompassed by your perfecting
will; through Jesus Christ who died and rose for us. *Amen.*

A Litany for the Discontinuing of Life-Sustaining Treatment: Form 2

The Minister introduces the litany with these or similar words

Hear, encourage, and strengthen us as we pray to you, Holy One, saying, "We put our trust in you."

As the centurion placed his sick servant under Jesus' authority, Holy One:
We put our trust in you.

As Jonah cried out from the belly of the fish, Holy One:
We put our trust in you.

As did the three young men in Nebuchadnezzar's fiery furnace, Holy One:
We put our trust in you.

As Gideon laid siege to his enemy with a tiny force, Holy One:
We put our trust in you.

As the sons of Zebedee left their father and their boat to follow Jesus, Holy One:
We put our trust in you.

As the magi followed the star, Holy One:
We put our trust in you.

As did Martha and Mary at the opening of Lazarus' tomb, Holy One:
We put our trust in you.

As Mary Magdalene released her risen Teacher, Holy One:
We put our trust in you.

The Minister adds the following or some other Collect

God our Wisdom: Bless the decisions we have made in hope, in sorrow, and in love; that as we place our whole trust in you, our choices and our actions may be encompassed by your perfecting will; through Jesus Christ who died and rose for us. *Amen.*

If Communion is not to follow, the service continues with the Lord's Prayer. The minister may introduce the prayer with these or similar words

As our Savior Christ
has taught us,
we now pray,

Our Father in heaven,
    hallowed be your Name,
    your kingdom come,
    your will be done,
        on earth as in heaven.
Give us today our daily bread.
Forgive us our sins
    as we forgive those
    who sin against us.
Save us from the time of trial,
    and deliver us from evil.
For the kingdom, the power,
    and the glory are yours,
    now and for ever. Amen.

And now, as our Savior
Christ has taught us,
we are bold to say,

Our Father, who art in heaven,
    hallowed be thy Name,
    thy kingdom come,
    thy will be done,
        on earth as it is in heaven.
Give us this day our daily bread.
And forgive us our trespasses,
    as we forgive those
    who trespass against us.
And lead us not into temptation,
    but deliver us from evil.
For thine is the kingdom,
    and the power, and the glory
    for ever and ever. Amen.

Laying on of Hands [and Anointing]

The minister may lay hands upon the person from whom treatment is to be withdrawn [and/or may anoint the person], pray silently, then pray aloud using one of the following forms or similar words

N., I lay my hands upon you in the name of our Lord Jesus Christ, beseeching him to uphold you and fill you with grace, that you may know the healing power of his love. *Amen.*

or this

N., I lay my hands upon you in the name of the Father, and of the Son, and of the Holy Spirit, trusting that God will do better things for you than we can desire or pray for. *Amen.*

or this

N., I lay my hands upon you [and anoint you] in the name of our Savior Jesus Christ. *Amen.*

An Act of Commitment

The service may continue with this act of commitment by family member(s) and/or friend(s) to the individual from whom treatment will be withdrawn.

The minister may introduce the act of commitment with these or similar words

Our Savior Jesus Christ chose to be like us in all things, even to sharing our suffering and death. As God is faithful to us, I now invite you to make a covenant of faithfulness with N.

Those present say

N., may Christ comfort you as you follow him on the path now set before you. With God's help, I will journey beside you. With

God's help, I will watch and wait with you, and with God's help, I will witness the love of Christ by my presence and prayers with you. Before God and your loved ones, I commit myself to you in the Name of Christ.

The Peace

All present may greet one another in the name of Christ.

If Communion does not follow, the service may conclude as follows

Minister	Into your hands, O Lord, I commend my spirit,
	For you have redeemed me, O God of truth.
People	Into your hands, O Lord, I commend my spirit.

Communion

If the Eucharist is to be celebrated, the Priest or Bishop begins with the Offertory.

If Communion is to be administered from the reserved Sacrament, the service continues with the Lord's Prayer, the minister first saying

As our Savior Christ
has taught us,
we now pray,

And now, as our Savior
Christ has taught us,
we are bold to say,

Our Father in heaven,
    hallowed be your Name,
    your kingdom come,
    your will be done,
        on earth as in heaven.
Give us today our daily bread.
Forgive us our sins

Our Father, who art in heaven,
    hallowed be thy Name,
    thy kingdom come,
    thy will be done,
        on earth as it is in heaven.
Give us this day our daily bread.
And forgive us our trespasses,

as we forgive those
who sin against us.
Save us from the time of trial,
and deliver us from evil.
For the kingdom, the power,
and the glory are yours,
now and for ever. Amen.

as we forgive those
who trespass against us.
And lead us not into temptation,
but deliver us from evil.
For thine is the kingdom,
and the power, and the glory
for ever and ever. Amen.

The minister may say the following Invitation

The Gifts of God for the People of God.

and may add

Take them in remembrance that Christ died for you, and feed on him in your heart[s] by faith, with thanksgiving.

The Sacrament is administered with the following or other words

The Body (Blood) of our Lord Jesus Christ keep you in everlasting life. [*Amen.*]

If the person cannot receive both the consecrated Bread and the Wine, it is suitable to administer the Sacrament in one kind only.

One of the usual postcommunion prayers is then said, or the following

Gracious Father,
we give you praise and thanks
for this Holy Communion
of the Body and Blood of your beloved Son Jesus Christ,
the pledge of our redemption;
and we pray that it may bring us forgiveness of our sins,
strength in our weakness,
and everlasting salvation;
through Jesus Christ our Lord. *Amen.*

or this

Faithful God
in the wonder of your wisdom and love
you fed your people in the wilderness with the bread of angels,
and you sent Jesus to be the bread of life.
We thank you for feeding us with this bread.
May it strengthen us
that by the power of the Holy Spirit
we may embody your desire
and be renewed for your service;
through Jesus Christ our Savior. *Amen.*

If a person desires Communion but is unable to eat and drink the Bread and
Wine, by reason of extreme sickness or disability, the minister should assure that
person that all benefits of Communion are received through an act of spiritual
communion even if the Sacrament is not received with the mouth. The minister
[and/or the individual who is ill] may pray, using these or similar words

Faithful God,
in the wonder of your wisdom and love
you fed your people in the wilderness with the bread of angels,
and you sent Jesus to be the bread of life.
Though *N.[I]* cannot consume these gifts of bread and wine,
we [I] thank you that *he/she has [I have]* received the sacrament
   of Christ's presence,
the forgiveness of sins, and all other benefits of Christ's passion.
By the power of the Holy Spirit,
may *we [I]* embody your desire
and be renewed for your service;
through Jesus Christ our Savior. *Amen.*

or this

God of infinite mercy,
we thank you for Jesus our Savior, our true Mother
who feeds us and gives us eternal life.
Though *N.[I]* cannot consume these gifts of bread and wine,
we [I] thank you that *he/she has [I have]* received the sacrament
   of Christ's presence,

the forgiveness of sins, and all other benefits of Christ's passion.
Grant that we may continue for ever in the Risen Life of our Savior,
who with you and the Holy Spirit,
lives and reigns, one God, now and for ever. *Amen.*

Grace

The Minister may conclude with one of the following

The grace of our Lord Jesus Christ, and the love of God, and the
fellowship of the Holy Spirit be with us all evermore. *Amen.*

or this

Glory to God whose power, working in us, can do infinitely more
than we can ask or imagine; glory to God from generation to
generation in the Church and in Christ Jesus for ever and ever.
Amen.

After this, treatment is withdrawn as needed.

*Ministration at the Time of Death may follow at a later time when death is
imminent.*

Additional Collects

For Health Care Providers

God, our Healer and Redeemer, we give thanks for the compassionate care N. has received. Bless these and all health care providers. Give them knowledge, virtue, and patience; and strengthen them in their ministry of healing and comforting; through Jesus Christ our Savior. *Amen.*

For All Who Suffer

O God, look with mercy on those who suffer, and heal their spirits, that they may be delivered from sickness and fear. Restore hope for the desolate, give rest to the weary, comfort the sorrowful, be with the dying; and bring them, finally, to their true heavenly home, for Jesus Christ's sake. *Amen.*

For One from Whom Treatment is to be Withheld or Discontinued

Holy God, whose peace passes all understanding, we pray that in your good time you will free N. from all earthly cares, pardon *his/her* sins, release *him/her* from pain, and grant that *he/she* may come to dwell with all your saints in everlasting glory, for the sake of Jesus Christ. *Amen.*

Burial of a Child

Burial of a Child

Concerning the Service

The death of a member of the Church should be reported as soon as possible to, and arrangements for the funeral should be made in consultation with, the Minister of the Congregation.

Baptized Christians are properly buried from the church. The service should be held at a time when the congregation has opportunity to be present.

The coffin is to be closed before the service, and it remains closed thereafter. It is appropriate that it be covered with a pall or other suitable covering. If necessary, or if desired, all or part of the service of Committal may be said in the church. If preferred, the Committal service may take place before the service in the church. It may also be used prior to cremation.

A priest normally presides at the service. It is appropriate that the bishop, when present, preside at the Eucharist and pronounce the Commendation.

It is desirable that the Lesson from the Old Testament, and the Epistle, be read by lay persons.

When the services of a priest cannot be obtained, a deacon or lay reader may preside at the service.

It is customary that the celebrant meet the body and go before it into the church or towards the grave.

The anthems at the beginning of the service are sung or said as the body is borne into the church, or during the entrance of the ministers, or by the celebrant standing in the accustomed place.

When children die, it is usually long before their expected span of life. Often they die very suddenly and sometimes violently, whether as victims of abuse, gunfire, or drunken drivers, adding to the trauma of their survivors. The surprise and horror at the death of a child call for a liturgical framework that addresses these different expectations and circumstances.

Gather in the Name of God

All stand while one or more of the following is said or sung

He will feed his flock like a shepherd; he will gather the lambs in his arms, and carry them in his bosom. *Isaiah 40:11*

The eternal God is your refuge, and underneath are the everlasting arms. *Deuteronomy 33:27*

As a mother comforts her child, so I will comfort you. *Isaiah 66:13a*

When Israel was a child, I loved him.... it was I who taught Ephraim to walk, I took them up in my arms.... I led them with...bands of love. I was to them like those who lift infants to their cheeks. I bent down to them and fed them. *Hosea 11:1a, 3, 4*

For these things I weep; my eyes flow with tears.... But you, O Lord, reign for ever; your throne endures to all generations. *Lamentations 1: 16a; 5:19*

Jesus said, Let the little children come to me, and do not stop them; for it is to such as these that the kingdom of heaven belongs. *Matthew 19:14*

For the Lamb at the center of the throne will be their shepherd, and he will guide them to springs of the water of life, and God will wipe away every tear from their eyes. *Revelation 7:17*

When all are in place, the Minister may address the congregation, acknowledging briefly the purpose of their gathering, and bidding their prayers for the deceased and the bereaved.

The Minister says one of the following Collects, first saying

	The Lord be with you.
People	And also with you.
Minister	Let us pray.

Silence

Holy God, your beloved Son took children into his arms and blessed them. Help us to entrust N. to your never failing loving-kindness. Comfort us as we bear the pain of *her/his* death, and reunite us in your good time in your Paradise; through Jesus Christ our Savior who lives and reigns with you and the Holy Spirit, one God, now and forever. *Amen.*

or this Collect for the family and all who grieve

Gracious God, we come before you this day in pain and sorrow. We grieve the loss of N., a precious human life. Give your grace to those who grieve [especially N.], that they may find comfort in your presence and be strengthened by your Spirit. Be with this your family as they mourn, and draw them together in your healing love; in the name of the one who suffered, died, and rose for us, Jesus our Savior. *Amen.*

The Lessons

One or more of the following passages from Holy Scripture is read. If the Eucharist is celebrated, a passage from the Gospel always concludes the Readings.

From the Old Testament

2 Samuel 12:16-23 (the death of David's child)
Isaiah 65:17-20, 23-25 (I am about to create new heavens and
  a new earth)
Isaiah 66:7-14 (As a mother comforts her child, so will I comfort you)
Jeremiah 31:15-17 (Rachel weeping for her children)

Psalms 23; 42:1-7

From the New Testament

Romans 8: 31-39 (Who will separate us from the love of Christ?)
1 Thessalonians 4:13-14,18 (We do not want you to be
  uninformed about those who have died)
1 John 3:1-2 (See what love the Father has given us)

Psalms 121; 139:7-12; 142:1-6

The Gospel

Matthew 5: 1-10 (Blessed are those who mourn)
Matthew 18: 1-5, 10-14 (this child is the greatest in the kingdom)
Mark 10:13-16 (Let the little children come to me); see also
Matthew 19:13-15; Luke 18:15-17
John 10:11-16 (I am the good shepherd)

The Sermon

*The Apostles' Creed may then be said, all standing. The Celebrant may
introduce the Creed with these or similar words*

In the assurance of eternal life given at Baptism, let us proclaim
our faith and say,

Celebrant and People

I believe in God, the Father almighty,
   creator of heaven and earth.
I believe in Jesus Christ, his only Son, our Lord.
   He was conceived by the power of the Holy Spirit
      and born of the Virgin Mary.
   He suffered under Pontius Pilate,
      was crucified, died, and was buried.
   He descended to the dead.
   On the third day he rose again.
   He ascended into heaven,
      and is seated at the right hand of the Father.
   He will come again to judge the living and the dead.

I believe in the Holy Spirit,
   the holy catholic Church,
   the communion of saints,
   the forgiveness of sins,
   the resurrection of the body,
   and the life everlasting. Amen.

The service continues with the Prayers. If the Eucharist is not celebrated, the Lord's Prayer concludes the intercessions.

The Prayers of the People

The Deacon or other person appointed says

In the peace of God, let us pray, responding "O God, have mercy."

In the assurance of your mercy, in thanksgiving for the life of your child N., and in confident expectation of the resurrection to eternal life, we pray

Here and after every petition, the people respond

O God, have mercy.

Remember N.'s parents, N. N. Help them to hold each other in their hearts, that this sorrow may draw them together and not tear them apart, we pray

Remember N.'s brother(s) N., N. and sister(s) N.,N., that *they/he/she* may be enfolded in love, comforted in fear, honored in *their/his/her* grief, and kept safe, we pray

Remember all the family and friends of N., that they may know the consolation of your love, and may hold N. in their love all the days of their lives, we pray

Support them in their grief, and be present to all who mourn, we pray

Teach us to be patient and gentle with ourselves and each other as we grieve, we pray

Help us to know and accept that we will be reunited at your heavenly banquet, we pray

Finally, our God, help us become co-creators of a world in which children are happy, healthy, loved and do not know want or hunger, we pray

The Minister concludes the prayers with this Collect

Compassionate God, your ways are beyond our understanding, and your love for those whom you create is greater by far than ours; comfort all who grieve for this child N. Give them the faith to endure the wilderness of bereavement and bring them in the fullness of time to share with N. the light and joy of your eternal presence; through Jesus Christ our Lord. *Amen.*

When the Eucharist is not to be celebrated, the service continues with the Commendation or with the Committal.

At the Eucharist

In place of the usual postcommunion prayer, the following is said

Almighty God, we thank you that in you great love you have fed us with the spiritual food and drink of the Body and Blood of your Son Jesus Christ, and have given us a foretaste of your heavenly banquet. Grant that this Sacrament may be to us a comfort in affliction, and a pledge of our inheritance in that kingdom where there is no death, neither sorrow nor crying, but the fullness of joy with all your saints; through Jesus Christ our Savior. *Amen.*

The Commendation

The Celebrant and other ministers take their places at the body.

This anthem, or some other suitable anthem, or a hymn, may be sung or said.

Give rest, O Christ, to your servant(s) with your saints,
where sorrow and pain are no more,
neither sighing, but life everlasting.

You only are immortal, the creator and maker of mankind; and we are mortal, formed of the earth, and to earth shall we return. For so did you ordain when you created me, saying, "You are dust, and to dust your shall return." All of us go down to the dust, yet even at the grave we make our song: Alleluia, alleluia, alleluia.

Give rest, O Christ, to your servant(s) with your saints,
where sorrow and pain are no more,
neither sighing, but life everlasting.

The minister, facing the body, says

We commend N. to the mercy of God, our maker, redeemer, and comforter.

N., our companion in faith and fellow child of Christ, we entrust you to God. Go forth from this world in the love of God who created you, in the mercy of Jesus who died for you, in the power of the Holy Spirit who receives and protects you. May you rest in peace and rise in glory, where pain and grief are banished, and life and joy are yours for ever. *Amen.*

or this

Into your hands, O merciful Savior, we commend your servant N. Acknowledge, we humbly beseech you, a sheep of your own fold, a lamb of your own flock, a sinner of your own redeeming. Receive *him* into the arms of your mercy, into the blessed rest of everlasting peace, and into the glorious company of the saints in light. *Amen.*

The Blessing and Dismissal follow.

The Committal

One or more of the following anthems is sung or said

They are before the throne of God,
and worship him day and night within his temple,
and the one who is seated on his throne will shelter them.
They will hunger no more and thirst no more;
the sun will not strike them, nor any scorching heat;
for the Lamb at the center of the throne will be their shepherd,
and he will guide them to springs of the water of life,
and God will wipe away every tear from their eyes.
Revelation 7:15-17

or this

See, the home of God is among mortals. He will dwell with them
   as their God;
they will be his peoples, and God himself will be with them;
he will wipe away every tear from their eyes. Death will be no more;
mourning and crying and pain will be no more, for the first
   things have passed away.
Those who conquer will inherit these things, and I will be their
   God, and they will be my children.
Revelation 21: 3b-4, 7

Before the following prayer, the coffin may be lowered into the grave.
Then, while earth is cast upon the coffin, the minister says these words

In sure and certain hope of the resurrection to eternal life through
our Lord Jesus Christ, we commend to Almighty God our *brother*
N., and we commit *his* body to the ground;* earth to earth, ashes
to ashes, dust to dust. The Lord bless *him* and keep *him,* the
Lord make his face to shine upon *him* and be gracious to *him,*
the Lord lift up his countenance upon *him* and give *him* peace.
Amen.

* *Or* the deep, *or* the elements, *or* its resting place.

Then shall be sung or said

Jesus said to his friends, "You have pain now; but I will see you
again, and your hearts will rejoice, and no one will take your joy
from you."
John 16:22

Then the minister says

        The Lord be with you.
People   And also with you.
Minister   Let us pray.

Loving God, we stand before you in pain and sadness. You gave the gift of new life, and now it has been taken from us. Hear the cry of our hearts for the pain of our loss. Be with us as we struggle to understand the mystery of life and death. Receive N. in the arms of your mercy, to live in your gracious and eternal love, and help us to commit ourselves to your tender care. In Jesus' name we pray. *Amen.*

or this

God, you have loved us into being. Hear our cries at our loss of N. Move us from the shadow of death into the light of your love and peace in the name of Mary's child, Jesus the risen one. *Amen.*

Here one or more of the additional prayers may be said. Then the Lord's Prayer may be said.

As our Savior Christ
has taught us,
we now pray,

And now, as our Savior
Christ has taught us,
we are bold to say,

Officiant and People

Officiant and People

Our Father in heaven,
   hallowed be your Name,
   your kingdom come,
   your will be done,
      on earth as in heaven.
Give us today our daily bread.
Forgive us our sins
   as we forgive those
   who sin against us.
Save us from the time of trial,
   and deliver us from evil.
For the kingdom, the power,
   and the glory are yours,
   now and for ever. Amen.

Our Father, who art in heaven,
   hallowed be thy Name,
   thy kingdom come,
   thy will be done,
      on earth as it is in heaven.
Give us this day our daily bread.
And forgive us our trespasses,
   as we forgive those
   who trespass against us.
And lead us not into temptation,
   but deliver us from evil.
For thine is the kingdom,
   and the power, and the glory
   for ever and ever. Amen.

The Blessing follows.

The God of peace, who brought again from the dead our Lord
Jesus Christ, the great Shepherd of the sheep, through the blood
of the everlasting covenant: Make you perfect in every good work
to do his will, working in you that which is well-pleasing in his
sight; through Jesus Christ, to whom be glory for ever and ever.
Amen.

The service concludes with this Dismissal

Since we believe that Jesus died and rose again, so will it be for
those who have died: God will bring them to life with Jesus.
Alleluia.

Go in peace in the name of Christ.

Additional Prayers

The Death of an Infant

God our Creator, you called into being this fragile life, which had seemed to us so full of promise: give to N., whom we commit to your care, abundant life in your presence, and to us, who grieve for hopes destroyed, courage to bear our loss; through Jesus Christ our Savior. *Amen.*

For a Miscarriage

O God, who gathered Rachel's tears over her lost children, hear now the sorrow and distress of N. [and N.] for the death of *their/her/his* expected child; in the darkness of loss, stretch out to *them/her/him* the strength of your arm and renewed assurance of your love; through your own suffering and risen Child Jesus. *Amen.*

For a Stillbirth or Child Who Dies Soon after Birth

Heavenly Father, your love for all children is strong and enduring. We were not able to know N. as we hoped. Yet you knew *her/him* growing in *her/his* mother's womb, and *she/he* is not lost to you. In the midst of our sadness, we thank you that N. is with you now. *Amen.*

For a Mother Whose Child has Died Near Birth

Loving God, we thank you that in your mercy you brought your daughter N. through childbirth in safety. We pray that N. [and N.] will know your support in this time of trouble and enjoy your protection always; through Jesus Christ our Savior. *Amen.*

For a Child Who Dies by Violence

Loving God, Jesus gathered your little ones in his arms and blessed them. Have pity on those who mourn for N., an innocent slaughtered by the violence of our fallen world. Be with us as we struggle with the mysteries of life and death; in our pain, bring your comfort, and in our sorrow, bring your hope and your promise of new life, in the name of Jesus our Savior. *Amen.*

or this

God our deliverer, gather our horror and pity for the death of your child N. into the compass of your wisdom and strength, that through the night we may seek and do what is right, and when morning comes trust ourselves to your cleansing justice and new life; through Christ our Savior. *Amen.*

or this

God, do not hide your face from us in our anger and grief for the death of N. Renew us in hope that your justice will roll down like mighty waters and joy spring up from the broken ground in a living stream; through Jesus our Savior. *Amen.*

For One Who has Killed

Holy God, we lift into the light of your justice N. [the one] who has taken the life of your child N. Where our hearts are stone return to us hearts of flesh; that grief may not swallow us up, but new life find us through Jesus the crucified, with whom we are raised by your power. *Amen.*

For Those Who Mourn

God of compassion and strength: keep safe the soul of your child N., whose moment of pain and fear is past. Send your healing to N. [and N.] and all who mourn, that their suffering may find peace and resolution within your love, whose Spirit gives life in Christ our Savior. *Amen.*

or this

Most loving God: the death of your Son has opened to us a new and living way. Give us hope to overcome our despair; help us to surrender N. to your keeping, and let our sorrow find comfort in your care; through the name and presence of Jesus our Savior. *Amen.*

or this

God, as Mary stood at the foot of the cross, we stand before you with broken hearts and tearful eyes. Keep us mindful that you know our pain, and free us to see your resurrection power already at work in *N.'s* life. In your time, raise us from our grief as you have raised N. to eternal life; through Jesus Christ our Savior. *Amen.*

or this

Merciful God, you grant to children an abundant entrance into your kingdom. In your compassion, comfort those who mourn for N., and grant us grace to conform our lives to *her/his* innocence and faith, that at length, united with *her/him,* we may stand in your presence in the fullness of joy; for the sake of Jesus Christ. *Amen.*

For a Child Dead by Suicide

Out of the depths we cry to you, merciful God, for your child N., dead by *her/his* own hand. Meet our confusion with your peace, our anger with forgiveness, our guilt with mercy, and our sorrow with consolation. Help us acknowledge the mystery that our lives are hid with Christ in you, whose compassion is over all whom you have made. *Amen.*

or this

All-knowing and eternal God, come to our help as we mourn for N., dead by *her/his* own hand. We know only in part, we love imperfectly, and we fail to ease one another's pain as you intend. But you are the God whose property is always to have mercy, and so we put our trust in you and ask the courage to go on; through our Savior Christ, who suffered for us, and whom you raised to new life. *Amen.*

Hymns Appropriate for the Burial of a Child

The Hymnal 1982

482	Lord of all hopefulness, Lord of all joy
490	I want to walk as a child of the light
620	Jerusalem, my happy home
645, 646	The King of love my shepherd is
676	There is a balm in Gilead
712	Dona nobis pacem

Wonder, Love, and Praise

787	We are marching in the light of God
800	Precious Lord, take my hand
810	You who dwell in the shelter of the Lord (Eagle's wings)
813	Way, way, way

Lift Every Voice and Sing II

8	Deep river
72	Just a closer walk with thee
91	Give me Jesus
103	Steal away
106	Take my hand
141	Shall we gather at the river
207	We'll understand it better by and by
213	Children of the heavenly Father
218	Jesus loves me, this I know
279	The Lord is my shepherd (Psalm 23)

Lutheran Book of Worship

474	Children of the heav'nly Father

Notes

Many of the prayers in "Ministry with the Sick or Dying" and "Burial of a Child" are from **The Book of Common Prayer 1979, The Book of Occasional Service, or Enriching Our Worship 1**. Others are adaptations from older sources, or from **The Book of Alternative Services** of the Anglican Church of Canada, **A New Zealand Prayer Book**, and **A Manual of Prayers and Readings for the Sick** by Norman Autton [SPCK, 1970]. There are also prayers written for these works, some submitted by consultants. Sickness, exhaustion, pain, and grief may often prompt the officiant to shorten prayers.

P. 25   *The Church's Teaching on Preparation for Death and Dying* was developed in consultation with the Episcopal Church's End-of-Life Issues Task Force, chaired by Cynthia Cohen. The section on "durable power of attorney" and "living wills" was drafted with legal advice from an Episcopal lawyer.

P. 28   The prayer beginning "God our healer..." is adapted from *All Desires Known* by Janet Morley [Morehouse Publishing, Harrisburg, *1992*, p. *5*]

P. 38   The exhortation beginning, "Holy Scripture teaches..." is adapted from the Canadian *Book of Alternative Services*, p. 555 *[see also p. 52]*.

The formula, "Receive Christ's gift of healing..." is adapted from *A New Zealand Prayer Book*, p. 743 *[see also p. 52]*.

P. 40   The phrase "Holy One of Blessing" originated in a Jewish congregation as a contemporary reformulation of the traditional Jewish invocation "Blessed are you, Lord our God, King of the universe" *[see also p. 54]*.

The prayer beginning "God of all mercy" acknowledges the Christian understanding that sickness is a universal condition, not, as this culture would often have it, an aberration, and that those who minister do not do so from a position of perfect health, but from the same weaknesses of the flesh to which the sick are vulnerable.

P. 41   The prayer beginning "Faithful God…" is based on John 6:32b-35, Christ as the bread of life, and Psalm 78:24-25, the retelling of that part of the Exodus story where God feeds the people in the wilderness with manna: "the grain from heaven. /So mortals at the bread of angels; /he provided for them food enough." Often, medical reasons preclude the sick from receiving the wine of the eucharist. This prayer emphasizes that the bread is sufficient *[see also pp. 56, 107, 125]*.

P. 57   The phrase, "Jesus…our true Mother," is derived from St. Anselm's Prayer 10 to St. Paul: *"Sed et tu Jesu bone domine, none tu mater, an non est mater qui tamquaqm gallina congret sub alles pullos suos? Vere domine, et tu mater. Nam et quod alii parturierunt et speperunt, a te accepterunt."* Dr. Eleanor McLaughlin translates this "But you O Jesus, good teacher, are you not also a mother, are you not that mother who as a mother hen gathers under her wings, her chickens? Truly Lord, you are also a mother because what others have conceived and given birth to they have received from you." This image possibly derives from St. Augustine who wrote of Psalm 101 [Vulgate], "Christ exercises fatherly authority and maternal love." The image appears in other patristic writings, as well. For instance, St. Bernard of Clairvaux tells a struggling novice, "[The Crucified] will be your mother, and you will be his son." Julian of

Norwich, throughout her *Showings* speaks repeatedly of divine motherhood, as when, in the 14th Showing, she says, *"Thus Iesus Christe that doith good agen evill is our very moder; we have our beyng of him wher the ground of moderhood begynnyth, with al the swete kepyng of love that endlessly folowith. As veryly God is our fader, as veryly God is our moder."* Canticles Q: "A Song of Christ's Goodness," and R: "A Song of True Motherhood," in the section entitled *Prayers for Use by a Sick Person [see pp. 91-92]*, translate the Anselm and Julian passages. The Anselm canticle is translated by the late Dr. Michael Vasey of the University of Durham, England. The Julian Canticle is translated by Br. Tristan, SSF. [For more on the imagery of Christ's motherhood, see "Lord, Teach Us to Pray: Historical and Theological Perspectives on Expanding Liturgical Language," by Paula S. Datsko Barker in *How Shall We Pray?* Church Publishing Incorporated, New York, 1994] *[see also pp. 107, 125. The phrase also appears in "A Litany for Healing" on p. 31]*.

The blessing beginning "May the God of hope fill you with every joy in believing" is adapted from *Celebrations for the Millennium* [Catholic Book Publishing Company, New Jersey, 1997].

P. 66   *For Protection* is from the Mozarabic rite *[see also p. 72]*.

P. 68   *For the Sleepless* has been adapted from a prayer in the Russian Orthodox Canon of Repentance *[see also p. 74]*.

P. 77   *In Loss of Memory*: In testimony at the 73rd General Convention, a gerontologist who composed this version of the prayer explained that people who are losing their memory need concrete naming and non-metaphorical language.

A Prayer of Thanksgiving for Caregivers is taken from words by Mechtilde of Magdeburg.

P. 78   *A Prayer of Comfort in God* is taken from words by Julian of Norwich.

In the first *Prayer After the Loss of a Pregnancy*, the scriptural source of Rachel's tears can be found in Jeremiah 31:15 and Matthew 2:18 *[see also p. 142]*. The second prayer recognizes that some people feel a residue of guilt, however blameless they may be for the miscarriage. Other women may have made a hard decision to end their pregnancy, yet grieve for the life that might have been, had circumstances been otherwise.

P. 95   In the prayer, *For Relatives of an Organ Donor*, the imagery of a grain of wheat is from John 12:24.

P. 108 The first commendation is adapted from *Revised Funeral Rites* [1997], published by the General Synod of the Episcopal Church in Scotland.

P. 111 The second prayer for release employs imagery from the Easter Vigil and the Baptismal Covenant.

A Litany Anticipating Heaven: The imagery in this litany derives from the hymn and preaching traditions of a variety of cultures, including the rich African-American heritage of images describing liberation and heaven.

"Gates of Paradise": 2 Esdras 4:7 speaks of the "gates of Paradise" which are also described at length in Revelation 21:12ff.

"Mercy-seat": Moses is instructed in Exodus 25:17 to make a mercy-seat over the Ark of the Covenant where God will be present. God is described as coming in clouds to the mercy-seat *[Leviticus 16:2]*. Christians have traditionally attached that name also to the throne of judgment on which the Son of Man will sit *[Matthew 19:28]* to judge the people at the renewal of all things, and to the throne of the Lamb *[Revelation 20-22]*. The image appears in the African-American hymn, "Come, Ye Disconsolate" *[see **Lift Every Voice and Sing II**, #147]*.

P. 112 "The welcome-table" encompasses God's "feast of fat things" as described in Isaiah 25:6, the banquet table of the king in the parables of Jesus *[Matthew 22:2]*, the feast of God's people to which the poor and outcast are specially to be invited *[Luke 14:13]*, and the feasting when Jesus the Bridegroom is present among his friends *[Matthew 9:15, Mark 2:19, Luke 5:34]*. It is a theme of African-American spirituals, as "I'm A-Going to Eat at the Welcome Table" *[see **Lift Every Voice and Sing II**, #148]*.

"The nuptial chamber" is the mystical place of the union of the soul with God *[Song of Solomon 1:4]* and, in an ancient tradition, Christ with his bride, the Church. In the parable of the wise and foolish virgins, the wise ones enter the nuptial chamber with the Bridegroom and the door is closed on their intimacy *[Matthew 25:1]*. This image was much developed in the monastic ascetic traditions of both Eastern and Western Christianity.

"The Supper of the Lamb": The marriage-supper of the Lamb is at the end-times *[Revelation 19:9]*, recalled in some fraction anthems *[see The Hymnal 1982, S172]* and the eucharistic feast of the Church, in general.

"The garden of delight" is the Garden of Eden, as described in Genesis 2:8. It is also identified with the secluded garden of marital union *[Song of Solomon 4:12-16, 5:1, 6:2]*. Zion restored from exile is to be a paradisal garden *[Isaiah 51:3; Hosea 14:7]*, the promised land is to be a garden for the people *[Genesis 13:10]*, and tradition links the garden of the tomb *[John 19:41]* in which Jesus was buried and where the risen Jesus met Mary Magdalene with the Garden of Eden and the paradisal garden-city of the New Jerusalem with its trees for healing the nations *[Revelation 22:2]*. The apocalyptic vision of 2 Esdras 7:36 describes the garden of delight open to the righteous.

"The lights of glory": The Wisdom of Solomon envisions the souls of the righteous at the time of their vindication as shining like sparks running through a field of stubble *[Wisdom 3:7]*. The Lord tells Ezra that, in the Messianic Age, the faces of those who have kept God's ways will "shine like the sun, and how they are to be made like the light of the stars, being incorruptible from then on" *[2 Esdras 7:97]*.

"Canaan-ground" is the promised land *[see also "land of milk and honey" below]* of Exodus 3:8 for the Israelites. It becomes the destination and camp-ground of God's people in resurrection, and a metaphor for heaven after they "cross over Jordan" in the language of such African-American spirituals as "Didn't My Lord Deliver Daniel" and "Go Down, Moses" *[see "To Jordan's other shore" p. 113]*.

P. 113 "The land of rest" is a place of observing Jubilee *[Exodus 23:11]*, the soul's place of rest *[Matthew 11:29]*, like a bird nesting on the horns of God's altar *[Psalm 116:6; 84:2]*, the tranquil destination of souls who have labored hard for the Gospel during life *[Hebrews 4:3, 10]*.

"The Holy City, the Bride" is drawn from the vision described in Revelation 21 and 22.

"The safe harbor": Psalm 107 speaks of God bringing the people safely "to the harbor they were bound for." Many poets including Gerard Manley Hopkins and John Masefield describe the journey to God as crossing the "harbor bar" into the "heaven-haven."

"The fount of life": Jesus is the fountain of living water springing up to eternal life *[John 4:14]*; God is the "fountain of life in which we see life" *[Psalm 36:9]*. The bride of The Song of Solomon (identified in some Christian traditions with Christ's Church) is described as "a garden fountain, a well of living water, and flowing streams from Lebanon" *[Song of Solomon 4:15]*. God is the people's fountain of living water in Jeremiah 2:13, and God will open a fountain of life in the Holy City of resurrection in Revelation 21:6.

"The gates of pearl": From Revelation 21:21, where the gates of the heavenly city are described as "twelve pearls, each of the gates is a single pearl."

"The ladder of angels": Jacob dreams of seeing a ladder to heaven *[Genesis 28:12]* on which angels ascend and descend. John 1:51 echoes this passage.

"The land of milk and honey" is referred to in Exodus 3:8 *[see "Canaan-ground" above]*.

"The clouds of glory" accompany the return of the Son of Man for judgment and triumph in Jewish apocalyptic literature, and also in Daniel 7:13, Matthew 24:30 and 26:64, Mark 13:26 and 14:62, and Luke 21:27, as well as Revelation 1:7. In the wilderness, the children of Israel saw God accompanying them as a pillar of cloud by day *[Exodus 13:22]* and as a cloud upon the holy mountain *[Exodus 19:9]*.

"The refreshing stream": See reference for "The fount of life" above, and also Psalm 46:5 and Isaiah 35:6;

66:12. The waters of God's refreshment ["I want a refreshing"] for the faithful are described in the Spiritual, "Grant Me a Blessing" *[Lift Every Voice and Sing II, #166]*. The hymn, "All Praise to You, O Lord," speaks of the "refreshing springs which you alone can give" *[The Hymnal 1982, #138]*.

P. 117 *passim. A Form of Prayer When Life-Sustaining Treatment is Withheld or Discontinued* has been adapted from "A Form of Prayer at a Time When Life-Sustaining Treatment is Withdrawn" in *Before You Need Them: Advance Directives for Health Care* [Forward Movement Publications, Cincinnati] with the permission of the Committee on Medical Ethics of the Diocese of Washington.

P. 120 *A Litany for the Discontinuing of Life-Sustaining Treatment: Form 2:* The centurion's sick servant is healed from afar by Jesus' authority in Luke 7:2ff. Jonah cries out from the belly of the fish in Jonah 2:1ff. The three young men in Nebuchadnezzar's fiery furnace trusted God and were delivered unharmed in Daniel 3. Gideon's triumph is described in Judges 7. The sons of Zebedee, James and John, leave their father to follow Jesus in Mark 1:20. The Magi following the star appears in Matthew 2. Martha and Mary witness the raising from the dead of their brother, Lazarus, in John 11. Mary Magdalene cannot hold on to her *Rabboni*—her teacher, the risen Jesus—as described in John 20:16.

P. 122-123 *An Act of Commitment* is inspired by a proposal in an article by the Rev. Peter A. Clark, S. J., published in *Worship*, July 1998, pp. 345-254.

P. 132 This translation of Deuteronomy 33:27 does not appear in the New Revised Standard Version of the Bible, but is derived from the Authorized Version. This phrase has traditionally been used in this form in other Anglican funeral services, most recently in the rite for the Burial of a Child in the new South African Prayer Book. [*See also "In Desolation" p. 78*].